IMAGES IN TIME

AUGUSTA
1868-1968

Images In Time
Augusta 1868 - 1968

ISBN 1-882420-31-4

First Printing, 1998
Printed in the United States of America
Produced by Hearth Publishing, Inc., Hillsboro, Kansas

COVER: The cover is a composite computer image combining a recent photograph of the interior of the museum (the original James Shamleffer General Store) with an old photograph of the Augusta Laundry delivery wagon. The historical photograph of the wagon was taken around 1880 in front of the former Opera House located on the south side of the 100 block on 5th street.

Cover photo by Stan Thiessen, Hearth Publishing.

FOREWORD

The Augusta Historical Museum began as a dream of Stella B. Haines, a well known Augusta resident and daughter of an early pioneer family. Realizing the importance of preserving history, she began collecting artifacts used by the early pioneer families and convinced the public school to give her a room where they could be viewed by the general public. Her next objective was to purchase and restore the log building which had been the James and Shamleffer General Store, the first building in the town. It took several years, a lot of hard work and dedicated volunteers, but by 1941, the log cabin was fully restored and open to the public. From that day forward, the museum has continued to grow. It now consists of not only the cabin, which is on the National Register of Historical Places, but also two other buildings. The main building houses displays, spanning from the 1860's through the 1940's. The museum, however, is not just a place for viewing, but has also accumulated numerous documents and resources covering topics of local history, microfilmed records, and family files for both historical and genealogical research. Thousands of people, both young and old, visit the museum yearly, where they can touch, see, and feel the lives of generations past and witness the development and growth of the area. It is the museum's purpose to protect, preserve, and exhibit artifacts from Augusta and the surrounding area. With that in mind, this pictorial history has been compiled from a portion of the museum's photograph collection, along with photographs submitted by individuals in the community. We hope you enjoy this trip through the past, from our meager beginnings of a trading post on the open prairie, to the introduction of the iron horse, the automobile, the discovery of gas and oil, and through times of war and times of celebration.

APPRECIATION

We wish to express our thanks to the people of Augusta who loaned their pictures to augment the Augusta Historical Museum's collection. We could not have published *Images In Time* without their help. A special thank you to Lucille Clingingsmith for her help in researching the material and Faye Teegarden for editing.

COMPILED BY

Virginia Belt and Doylene Foreman

SPONSORS

A special "Thank You" to the page sponsors who made this book possible.

Augusta Historical Museum Executive Director and Curator: Doylene Foreman

Augusta Historical Society, Board Of Directors, 1998-99:

PRESIDENT, Gary Agard

VICE-PRESIDENT, Melanie Tennyson

SECRETARY, Jane Mathias

TREASURER, Melissa Davidson

DIRECTORS:

Harold Arnold — Virginia Belt — Robert Bisagno

Bruce Bourget — George Mabry — Sherman Parry

Bill Shriver — Raymond Teegarden

▲ The Shamleffer and James General Store was the first building erected in the city of Augusta. Built in 1868, it stood 1 1/2 stories tall and was constructed of hand-hewn logs from along the Walnut River. Some of these logs are 12" to 14" in width. Augusta's first school classes were held in the upper loft and it became the meeting place of the Baptist and Methodist churches and the Masonic Lodge. It also was a stop along the stagecoach route and the location of the first post office. The general store, often referred to as a trading house in the 1870's, proved to be a success. In the first 15 months of business, over $60,000.00 in goods were sold.

▲ Shamleffer and James eventually sold the general store to Thomas Stewart and Co., who continued to operate the store until the mid 1870's. In 1878, siding was placed over the logs of the cabin and the roof was raised to make a full second story. Over the next 40 years, various families owned the cabin and made it their home. One of these was the Winters family and, although it is not documented, it is told that their son Gus was born in the cabin. In 1923 and 1924 it was divided into 6 rooms on each floor and became known as the Dad Sparger Boarding House, for men only. Some years later, it was a furniture and woodworking shop owned by Gene Schultz. In 1940 , the Augusta Historical Society purchased the cabin, removed the siding, and restored it to its original appearance. The cabin remains today in its original location at 303 State St., and is on the National Register of Historical Places.

1868-1880

Sponsored by Gary and Norma Agard and by George R. and Jean Mabry

▲ Chester N. James, Augusta's town founder, co-owned the Shamleffer and James General Store. He came to Butler County, in 1868, at the age of 32. He and Mr. Wm. Shamleffer purchased 80 acres of what is now downtown Augusta, for $40.00. Mr. James, who managed the store, established the Augusta Post Office and served as Postmaster for six years. He took an active role in the organization of both the Baptist Church and the Masonic Lodge. Instrumental in all aspects of the town's development, he became Augusta's first Mayor and was Superintendent of School for six years. He also served as Justice of the Peace and was elected Clerk of the District Court for four consecutive years. Mr. James and his wife moved from the area sometime in the mid 1880's.

▲ Augusta James, wife of Chester N. came to Butler County with her husband in 1868. When it became time to establish a Post Office, it was realized that the settlement would need a name. An election was held and Augusta took the honor. It is said her name was chosen because of her generosity and friendliness to all. She was very involved in the Baptist Church and no doubt assisted Mr. James in the general store.

▲ The first house in Augusta was built by Mr. James for himself and his wife. Located on the southwest corner of 4th and State, it was almost entirely constructed of lumber from the Palmer Saw Mill, which had recently located on the west bank of the Walnut River. In the mid 1870's it became the home of L.N. Blood (clerk and school teacher) and his new bride, Leonora Bellamy.

◀ William "Billy" Shamleffer was part owner of the Shamleffer and James General Store. A businessman, he made his home in Council Grove, Kansas, where he engaged in a similar type of operation. Although he never lived in Augusta, he was activily involved in the establishment of the store and was the financial backer for much of the land.

▲ Leonard Shamleffer, younger brother of Billy, helped construct the Shamleffer and James General Store, along with J.L. Sharp and John Herman Walworth (whose family eventually settled in the area). Once the cabin was completed, Leonard, who was 17 years old, remained to guard the building until Mr. James arrived with the supplies. For three months he waited, each day saddling his pony and riding up the hill north of town. There he would spend hours looking for the expected wagons. Following Mr. James arrival, Leonard returned to Council Grove. In later years, he was to settle in the Douglas area.

▲ L.N. Blood came to Augusta in 1869, and was employed as a teacher for the first school classes. There were 46 students enrolled with an average attendance of 30. The first classes were held in the upper loft of the Shamleffer and James General Store. When not teaching, Mr. Blood worked as a clerk in the store and became assistant Postmaster. As assistant postmaster, he was required to arise from his bed at 2:00a.m., hearing the blast from a horn blown by the driver of an approaching stagecoach. Mr. Blood would then turn over the outgoing mail to the driver. In the spring of 1871, Mr. Blood engaged in the mercantile business for himself, opening a store further north on State street. In 1883, he went to St. Louis, Mo. where he became a well known and prosperous broker. While his business activities took him away from Butler County, he returned each year and maintained important financial interests in the area.

▲ The first meat market and bakery in Augusta. The exact location of these buildings is unknown.

◀ Leonora Bellamy came to Butler County in 1869 and opened a milliner shop. Pictured here in her wedding dress, she married L.N. Blood on July 2, 1871. Soon after they made their home in the house at 4th and State (pictured previously in this book). Leonora was the first donor toward the restoration of the log cabin in 1940 and her wedding glove and fan are on display at the Augusta Museum, along with the table lamp used while she and L.N. were courting.

▲ Henry Moyle came to Augusta in 1869 where he met and married Josephine Sanders in 1873. He was a partner in the hardware business and opened a grocery store in 1878. Henry was active in all Augusta endeavors and served as Mayor for a number of terms. Many of his children went on to serve in positions of prominence in the area. Pictured here are members of the Henry Moyle family; (Standing L.to R). Grace Moyle-Skaer, Harry Moyle, Matt Moyle, John Moyle, Beaulah Moyle-Alexander. (Seated L to R) Josephine Sanders Moyle, Fanny Moyle, and Henry Moyle.

Sponsored by John and Marilyn Mardis Huston

▲ W.A. Shannon worked as a receiver for the land office when it opened in Augusta on October 1, 1870. He became quite active in the real estate business and in the development of Augusta. He soon took the position of Justice of the Peace and also served on the Augusta City Council.

▲ Dr. M.R. Bruce was a physician in Augusta from 1877 to 1887. This photo was taken of him in 1865, while serving as a soldier in the Civil War.

▲ Augusta Physician, Dr. Samual A. Davis, is pictured here in his office. The calendar on the wall is dated October, 1878.

◀ George and Caroline Skaer arrived in Augusta in 1874. George built a small house in the 300 block of State Street across from the present Augusta Museum. Shortly thereafter, he commenced constructing the family home, one mile east of Augusta on the south side of what is presently U.S. Highway 54. Many of their children were involved in retail businesses, banking, and the oil industry. Pictured here are (Back Row L to R) James Skaer, Gus Skaer, Walter Skaer, Albert Skaer, Arthur Skaer, John Skaer, Ed Skaer. (Front Row L to R) William Skaer, Caroline Skaer McVay, George Skaer, Caroline Seibert Skaer, Henry Skaer.

Sponsored by Joan Winzer Snyder

▲ Mr. S.J. Safford came to Butler county in 1879 and engaged in the lumber business. Shown here is both an exterior (Mr. Safford is on the far right) and interior picture of their very first building located on the corner of sixth and School. The lumber company, which was passed down to Mr. Safford's son, Eugene and then his son, Edward and eventually a son-in-law, Lee Hoopes, remained an active business in Augusta until the mid 1970's.

Sponsored by William Morris Associate Architects, 112 E. 5th

1880-1890

▲ The first railway to cross through Augusta was the Frisco Railroad in 1880. Shown here is the station in the late 1800's, before an addition was added to the building. The station remains today in its original location at 628 State Street. Note the J.C. Haines Grain Company in the background.

▲ The Atchison, Topeka and Santa Fe lines came to Augusta in 1881. This frame building served as its first depot, located on its present site at 5th and Osage.

Sponsored by Augusta Animal Clinic, 704 Belmont

▲ The south side of the 100 block of east 5th street was known as the Opera Block, from 1882 through the turn of the century. Built by A. Kuster, it was a two story native stone building which stretched from east to west along the south side of 5th street. The far east end was occupied by the George Brown Bank. On west, was Worden & Wishard, followed by several other retail businesses. The upper story of the building was the Opera House, for which the block was named.

◀ On any given evening, you might have seen gentlemen dressed in cutaway frocks with fancy worsted vests, and ladies in long flowing gowns, felt plumed hats, and elbow length gloves entering the Opera House. It was not only a large hall, but also one of the most elaborate, modern and fully equipped stage theaters of its time. It had a seating capacity of 500 and was used for traveling and local plays, concerts, elaborate balls, weddings, and commencement exercises. In 1888 it was sold to Mr. S.G. Hindman. Currently on display at the Augusta Historical Museum is a lamp globe which hung in the Opera House and two of its original chairs.

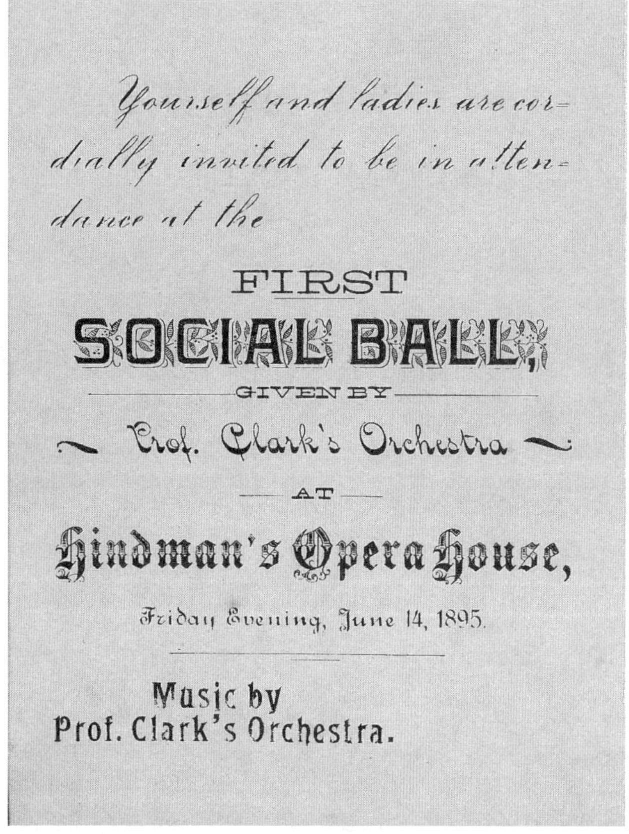
Yourself and ladies are cordially invited to be in attendance at the

FIRST
SOCIAL BALL,
GIVEN BY
Prof. Clark's Orchestra
AT
Hindman's Opera House,
Friday Evening, June 14, 1895.

Music by
Prof. Clark's Orchestra.

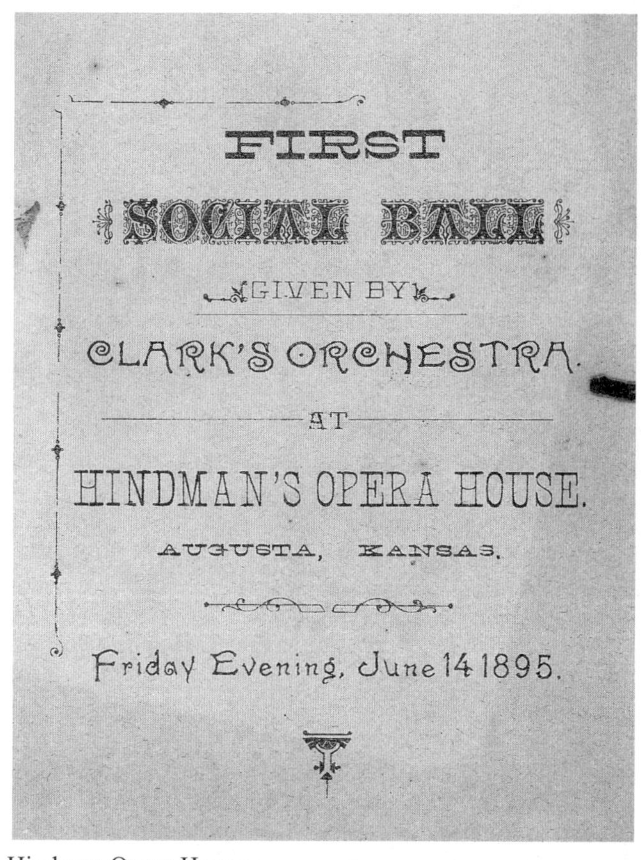
FIRST
SOCIAL BALL
GIVEN BY
CLARK'S ORCHESTRA.
AT
HINDMAN'S OPERA HOUSE.
AUGUSTA, KANSAS.

Friday Evening, June 14 1895.

▲ An invitation to attend a Social Ball on June 14, 1895, at the Hindman Opera House

◄ The first graduate of the Augusta School System was Atta Wishard in 1881.

Sponsored by Senator and Mrs. David R. Corbin

▲ In the late 1800's, the 500 block of State Street acquired the nickname of Horseshoe Block. In the middle of the street you can see the Town Well. Some say that an indentation from the well remains in the street today. Note the horseshoe on the front of the brick building across the street.

▲ Erasmus Johnson's Livery Stable, 1880 to 1885

▲ The interior of an Augusta store in the late 1800's. The name and location of the store is unknown.

Sponsored by Sharp Realty, 430 Walnut - Walt Sharp, Craig Sharp, & Tamara Cook

▲ John W. Skaer's Hardware and Buggies store.

▲ The Boyle Hotel stood on the southwest corner of 7th and State. In later years it became the Arthur Skaer family home. In 1929, it was moved to the east end of 7th street and was torn down when the overpass was built.

▲ This is a calendar top from the late 1800's, featuring the interior of the Chance and Bigger Store

▲ The Augusta Band posed for a photo on July 4, 1888, when they were performing for the Annual 4th of July Celebration.

▲ The City Steam Mills was a flour mill owned by A.J. and J.W. Grounds, who came to Augusta in 1879. The mill was located in the southeast portion of town adjacent to the Santa Fe Railroad. This photo was taken of the Walnut River running over its banks and moving in toward the building during the 1889 flood.

Sponsored by Walt and Jackie Sharp

▲ The flood of 1889 washed out the Walnut Bridge south of town and left only ruins in place of a lumber mill, located on the west banks of the Walnut River.

▲ In August of 1889, a new bridge was completed across the Walnut, replacing the one destroyed in the recent flood. Some of the workman posed for this picture along the edge of the bridge.

Sponsored by Stevens Lumber Co., Douglas, Ks., - Glenn and Norma Stevens, owners

▲ A view of south State Street, looking North, in the late 1880's.

▲ The J.C. Haines home, 609 School Street in 1880-90. During that time, many families rented out rooms in their homes. A sign on the door appears to read "Boarding House".

▲ The interior of an Augusta home in the late 1800's.

Sponsored by Kerry Unrein Painting and Signs, 616 Walnut

▲ H. V. Butcher was Superintendant of Augusta Schools from 1893 to 1896. He later became a newspaper editor in Caldwell, Kansas.

▲ Jacob Beck was the county's first mail carrier. The photo is signed "Given to Maggie by Jake, Aug. 2, 1893".

◀ The Fifth Avenue Hotel opened in the late 1800's. Ranked as a first class hotel, it was described as offering a lavish but comfortable setting. The frame building, located on the northwest corner of 5th and School, was destroyed by fire and in 1913 a new stone structure was built in its place. The stone building remains today.

Sponsored by Ralph and Virginia Ward Belt and by Rod and Melissa Burress Davidson

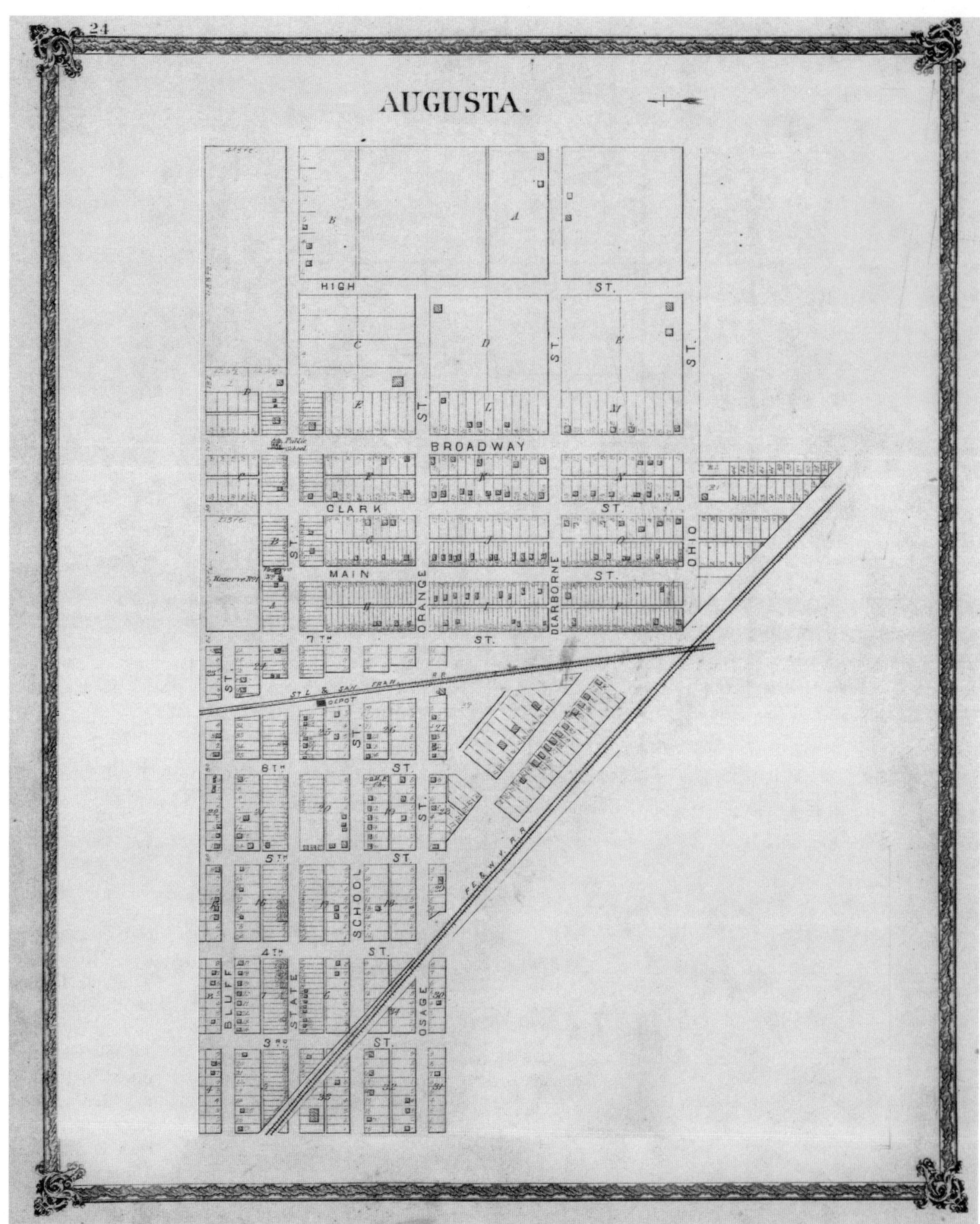

▲ 1885 Plat of the city of Augusta

▲ The Elm Creek Anti Horse Thieving Association was organized under jurisdiction of the law in the early 1880's, to pass along information about strangers under suspicion of livestock theft. They would trail such individuals and take whatever actions were necessary to recover the livestock and return it to its owners. The Vigilantes and Regulators were forerunners to the association; however, they worked outside the law, while the association worked with the blessing of authorities. Only four of the men shown here are identified: 2nd from the left is Frank Buffum; 5th from the left, Grant Holmes; far right is Henry Boucher, and 4th from the right, Jim Shreve.

▲ A bandstand stood in the city park which was located on the west side of the 500 block of School Street. Posing in front of the bandstand are members of the Bicycle Club of 1896.

▲ The photo is part of a calendar top, dated 1896, showing the interior view of the Peckham and McIlvain store, located at 501 State. The store was opened in 1893 by W.W. Peckham and carried everything from clothing to carpet.

◀ George Ohmart is shown here in front of his Blacksmith Shop on the east side of the 600 block of Walnut Street. George also served many years as Justice of the Peace.

Sponsored by Fletcher's Barber Shop, 505 State St. - Dennis and Anna Fletcher

▲ The center building marked "Grain" is the same building used for the first school. The two-room frame structure was built in 1870 in the 500 block of School street. In 1880 when a new school was constructed, the frame building was moved and used for church services by the Presbyterian Congregation. In 1899, the frame building was once again moved to the J.C. Haines Company in the 600 block of school street.

▲ A group of young Augusta girls enjoying some watermelon on a summer's afternoon, in the 1890's.

▲ The Lincoln School was built in 1881 at 917 State Street. All grades attended classes in the two-story stone structure. Although other schools were eventually built in addition to the Lincoln, it continued to be used until it was torn down in 1938 to make room for the new Junior High.

▲ Students, teachers, and parents survey the damage, after a cyclone ripped off the roof of the Lincoln School Building in 1902.

Sponsored by Farm Bureau Insurance, 213 W. 7th, Martha M. Walker, Agent

1900-1910

▶ Augusta's first soda fountain was installed in the Smith Drug Store in June, 1900. It was an eight syrup fountain about 30 inches long and was iced from the top under the canopy. The sides were marble, and the front onyx; and the canopy, oak. The fountain was made by O. Counsil of Augusta, at a cost of $900.00. Water was carried from a cistern in the rear of the store and the glasses were washed in pans and buckets. Coca-Cola was served from the urn shown on the counter. The fountain shut down in the fall and opened again in the spring. Ice cream sodas were priced at a nickel.

▲ In 1902, the A.E. Schultz Grocery store was located at 420 State Street.

Sponsored by Shryock Oil Co., 415 W. 7th

▲ In the 1900's, the Viets Clothing Co. was one of the most popular mens and boys clothing stores in the area. Located at 429 State Street, it became famous for its three clothed mannequins placed outside in front of the store. They were always dressed according to the weather, wearing such things as: rain coats and slickers when it rained, coats and gloves when it snowed. A cord was stretched across the front of the store where pants and shoes were hung. Among the goods inside one could find suits ranging from $5.00 to $15.00, never hung, but piled on tables. In 1917, the front of the store was remodeled and a second story was added. Then the building to the north was purchased and a ladies ready-to-wear and dry goods store was added. In later years the north building was sold and Calverts Department Store was opened.

Sponsored by Early Bird, Etc, 312 W. 7th - Terry Kidd, owner

▲ George Brown came to Augusta in 1870 and opened a bank in a two-story frame building in the 100 block of 5th street. In 1882, the building was destroyed by fire and the Kuster Opera Block was erected in its place. Mr. Brown's bank occupied the east end of the Kuster building until after the turn of the century, when it was moved to 501 State Street. Shown here is the interior of their new facility on State Street.

◀ Augusta Baseball Team in 1905. (Front Row, L to R) Earl Leppelman, Bill Watt, John Cox, Frank Steiger; (middle row, L to R) Clint Smith, Bert Brown, R.W. Stephenson, Clyde Paul, Burton Ayres, and Herb Crane ;(back row, L to R) Lewis "Doc" Jones, Deering Marshall.

Sponsored by Augusta Tire and Auto Supply, Inc., 522 W. 7th

▲ Threshing machine, early 1900's.

▲ In 1905, the W.W. Peckham Mercantile was located at 423 State Street.

Sponsored by Novaks Glass Shop, Inc., 700 State St. - Carol and Johnny Novak

▲ The Herb Hamblet Barber Shop was located in the basement of the building on the northeast corner of 5th and State in 1907. Barber Bert Brown is shown standing next to the far left chair; Barber Fred Fletcher is standing at the middle chair, and the man seated in the middle with his back to the camera is H. Hamblet, owner of the shop. C.N. Hamblet, the oldest son of H.H., is wearing the long coat and standing next to the far right chair. A calendar is placed on the ceiling for the convenience of the shave customers, along with calendars from Paul and Penley Hardware and the First National Bank. The wall is covered with postcards, and lard can lids are placed above the gaslights for heat reflectors.

▲ Going south on Osage between 7th and Main, are Ernest and Mary West in their common mode of travel, the horse and buggy.

1910-1920

▲ The Augusta Gazette building in October of 1910.

▼ Looking south in the 500 block of State street, in 1910. The streets had not yet been paved.

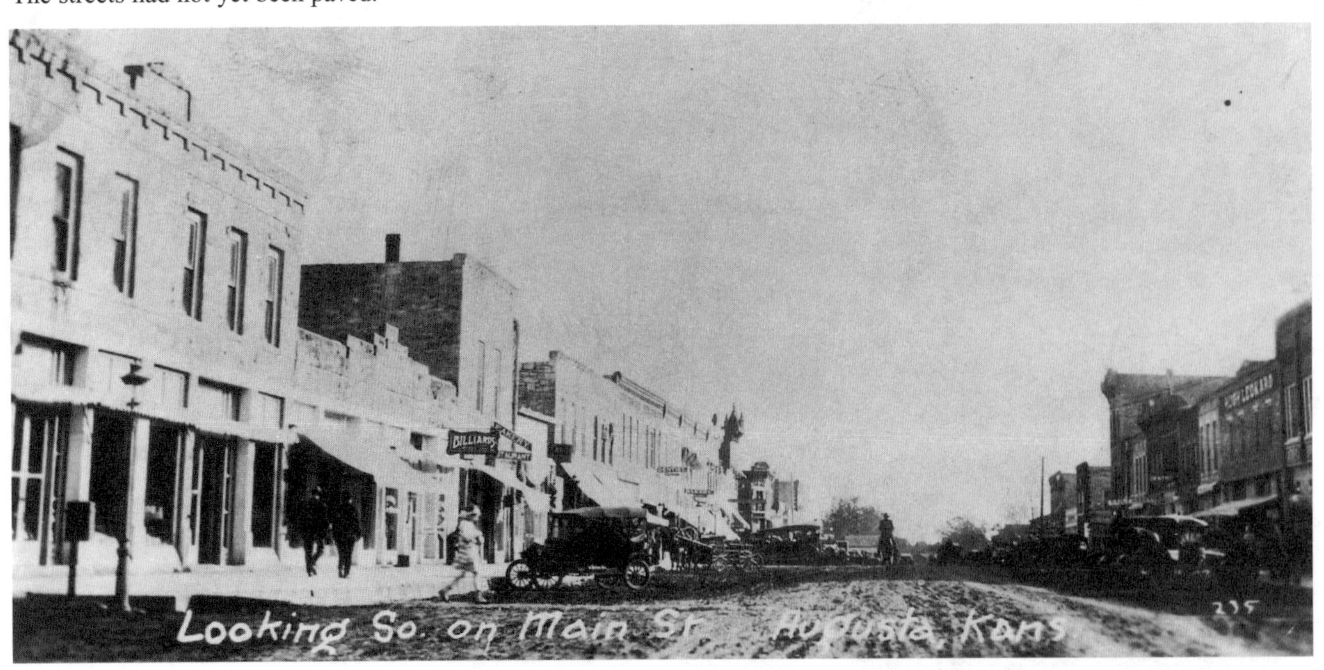

Sponsored by Plaza IGA, 303 W. 7th - Tim and Toni Voegeli, owners

▲ Looking south in the 600 block of State street. The first building on the far right has been destroyed by fire. The next building south, was built by John Moyle in 1918, and has been the location of such hotels as the Royal, Plains, and Holland House. Next you can see the five-story Moyle Building, built by Henry Moyle in 1915.

▲ Henry Lichliter's threshing machine and crew in 1910.

Sponsored by Keith and Jan Shriver Scholfield

▲ Frisco Band, 1911

▲ The Victory Glass Factory, located at the railroad junction, opened in 1914. Its primary product was window glass. The building was destroyed during the 1924 tornado and the factory never reopened. The Augusta Museum has on display, several glass dippers, canes, and bowls, made by the factory workers.

Sponsored by, Augusta Pharmacy, Augusta Plaza Shopping Center - Ron Chiaro, RPH

▲ Victory Glass Factory workers in 1914.

▲ Pictured here in 1917 is the Walnut Oil Refinery. It was one of the first three refineries established in Augusta (the others being the Lakeside Refinery and the White Eagle Refinery). Built by Clemens and Lavery from Oklahoma, it was located south of town, just across the tracks on the east side of the road. It was later bought by White Eagle.

▲ This is one of the Walnut River Filling Stations affiliated with the Walnut Refinery.

▲ Some dapper gents of the 1910's. (L to R) Francis and Cecil Skaer, Stanley Ayres, Waldo Busby, Walter Skaer, Clarence Hamblet.

Sponsored by Bob Monroe Law Offices, 425 State St.

▲ The telephone company staff posed for a picture in 1915. (Back Row) Myrtle Pimlot and Charles Bankey, Telephone installer; (Front Row) Cecil Schultz, Mrs Easley, Margaret Clark, Minnie Clark.

▲ A.E. Schultz, who operated a grocery store at 319 State Street, shows off his Iten Biscuit display which appeared in the Merchant's Journal in 1915.

Gabler & Brannon Rig Building Gang For Empire Gas & Fuel Co
Starting To Work. Augusta Ks. Oil Fields.

▲ The Gabler & Brannon rig building gang, for the Empire Gas & Fuel Co., lined up in the 400 block of State Street on the day they were beginning work in the Augusta Oil Fields.

▲ A bird's-eye view of the back side of State Street in the 1000 block, looking northeast. On the right is the old high school, built in 1911 on the corner of High and State.

Sponsored by Mark and Kay McCollom

▲ Nathan Rich Chance and Mary Emily McKnight Chance moved into this house on the corner of Clark and Dearborn in 1916 and lived there until 1933.

Sponsored by The Bisagno Family

▲ A storm had been brewing for sometime, in October of 1916, when the citizens of Augusta became enraged with the local police officers, known as the Crowe Brothers. The officers had jailed several residents for trivial matters and had persecuted the citizens rather than protecting them. After some individuals were jailed for no tail lights, an Augusta resident, W.R. Peal, decided to take action. He mounted a horse and headed down the street, holding as a tail light, a lantern at the end of a pole. The officer walked behind him and shot eight times in the air. When he started to arrest Peal, the crowd went wild. They chased the officers down the block, until they disappeared. The citizens then battered in the jail and seventeen prisoners were released.

Sponsored by Michael Clifton, CPA, 605 State St.

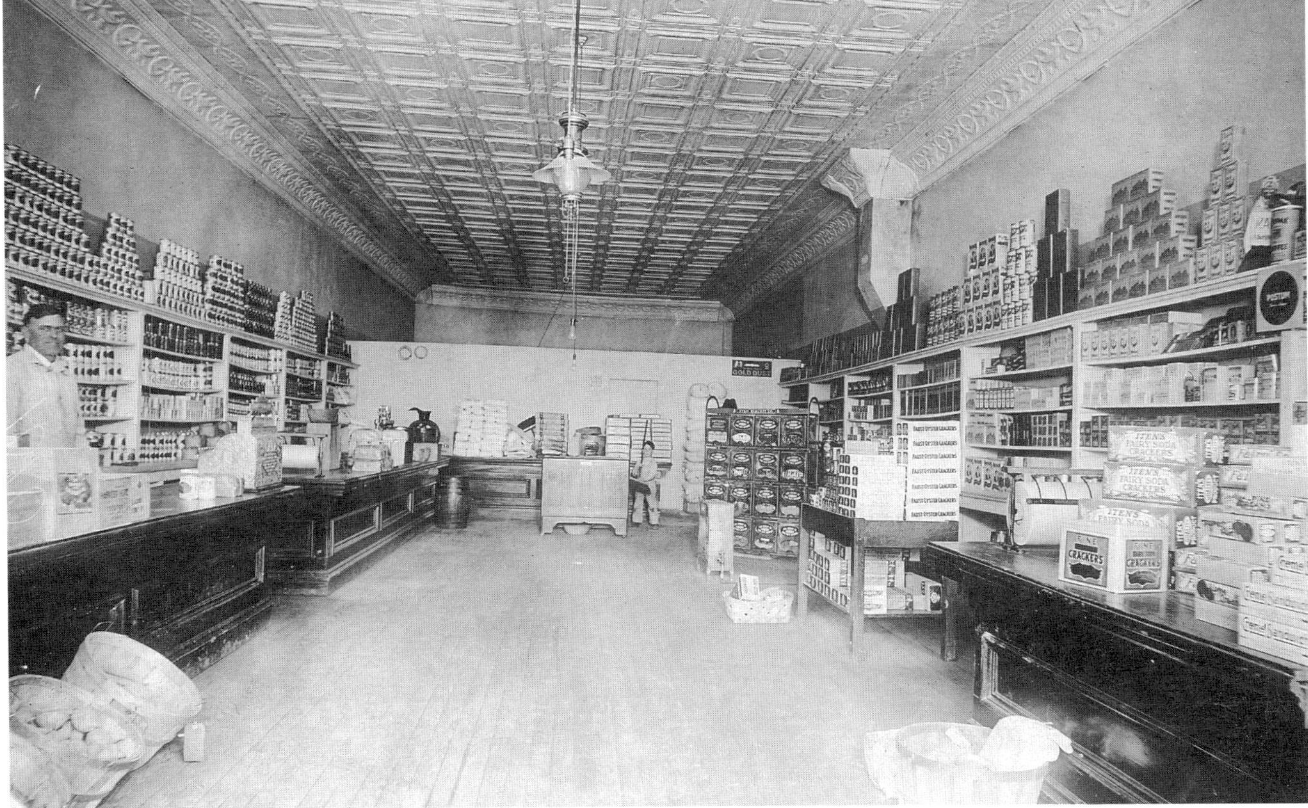

▲ The Samuel G. Grimes family settled in Augusta in 1916. Upon arriving, they took shelter in their tent and covered wagon until they found a home. In 1919 they opened the Samuel Grimes & Sons Grocery Store at 607 State St.

▲ A Baggage-Transfer Wagon owned by Jas. Starkey, was stopped in front of the Frick Reed Supply. Mr. Starkey ran his business out of his home at 609 Walnut.

▲ The Economy Grocery at 420 State Street opened in 1918. Shown here are Harvey Brown, Spencer Ryan, Charlie Kontz, unknown, Mr. Moore.

Sponsored by Sigma Tek, Inc., Instruments and Avionics, 1001 Industrial Rd.

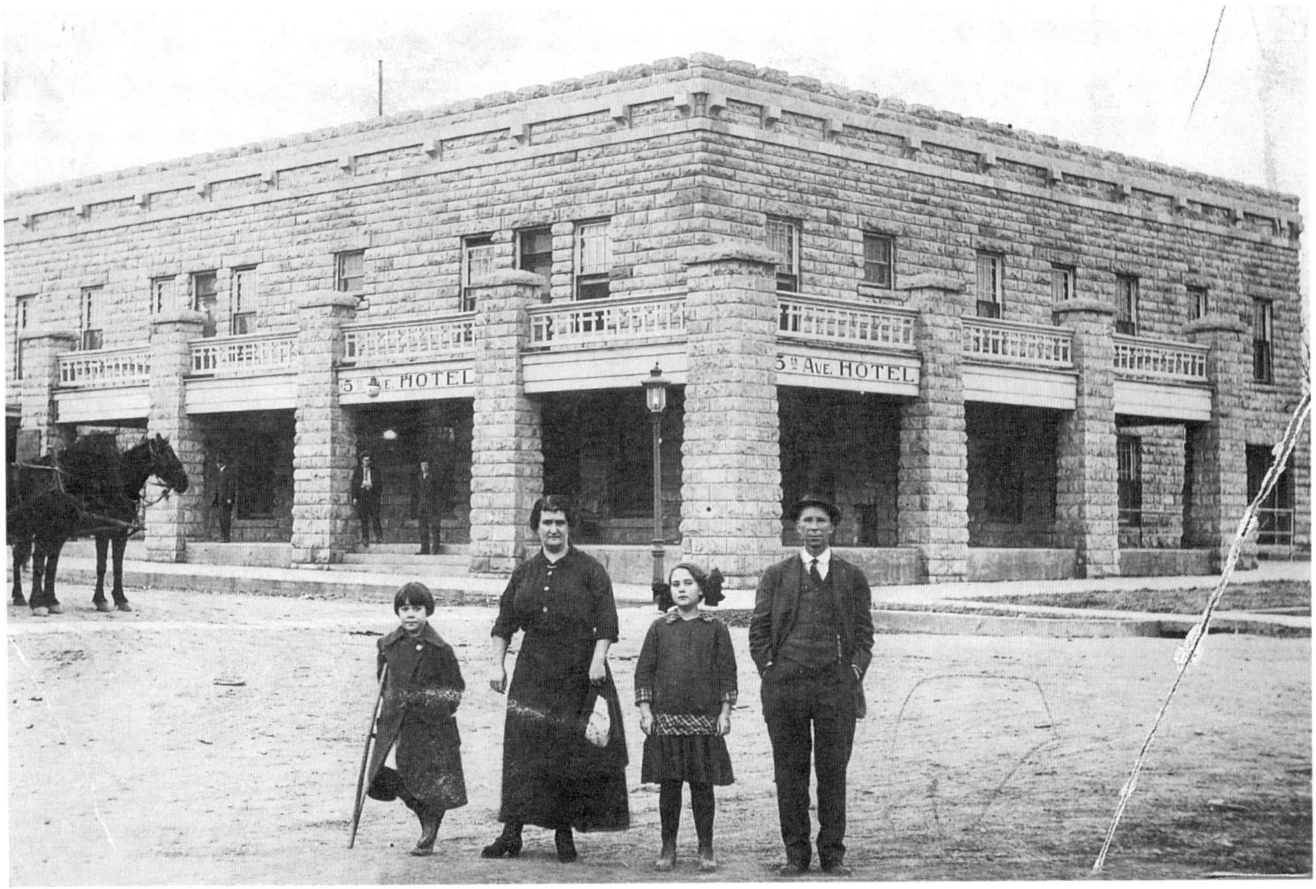

▲ In 1913, a new Fifth Avenue Hotel was built on the northwest corner of 5th and School, in place of the hotel's two-story frame building which had recently burned.

◀ Orville Long (left) and John Neff (right) stand at the lobby desk of the 5th Avenue Hotel. Along the wall, is a crank telephone, campaign poster for Woodrow Wilson, and a calendar giving the date of February, 1913. A glass case holds cigars and tobacco papers for the guest and a sign on the back wall reads "clothing cleaned & pressed overnight". A large railroad map of the Atchison, Topeka & Santa Fe lines hangs on the back wall, to assist travelers.

▲ The Moyle Building, on the northwest corner of 6th and State, was the tallest building in Augusta. Built by Henry Moyle in 1915, it stood five stories high. The upper floors were filled with offices of various companies, doctors and oil businesses, while the Grand Leader Mercantile Company occupied the street level. The building remains today, however, the top two levels were destroyed by the 1924 tornado and never replaced.

◀ The oil boom came to Augusta in the early 1910's. By 1917, there were three refineries located in the area. Here is a view of the original White Eagle Petroleum Co.Refinery. Although the other refineries did not survive, the White Eagle continued in operation until 1930, when it was purchased by Standard Oil Co. of New York (Socony), then two years later, Socony merged with Vacuum Oil Co. and became Socony-Vacuum. In 1966 the refinery was bought by the Mobil Oil Corporation.

▲ Augusta Oil fields, south of town.

▲ Even as today, the tow truck business was prosperous in the late 1910's. The phone number listed on the truck belonged to A. Harrison, who lived on Santa Fe street.

Sponsored by LakePoint Nursing Center, 901 LakePoint Drive

1920-1930

▲ In the early 1900's, banker Warren E. Brown built a large, elegant home for himself and his wife, Ivy at 619 Santa Fe. When the Brown's moved to Wichita, the home was chosen as the site for the first Augusta Hospital. The hospital opened its doors to the public on December 12, 1920, under the leadership of Dr. J.C. Bunten. In early 1922, the building was enlarged by a substantial addition. The hospital had a twenty four bed capacity and the best equipment obtainable.

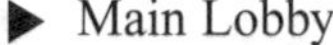

▶ Main Lobby

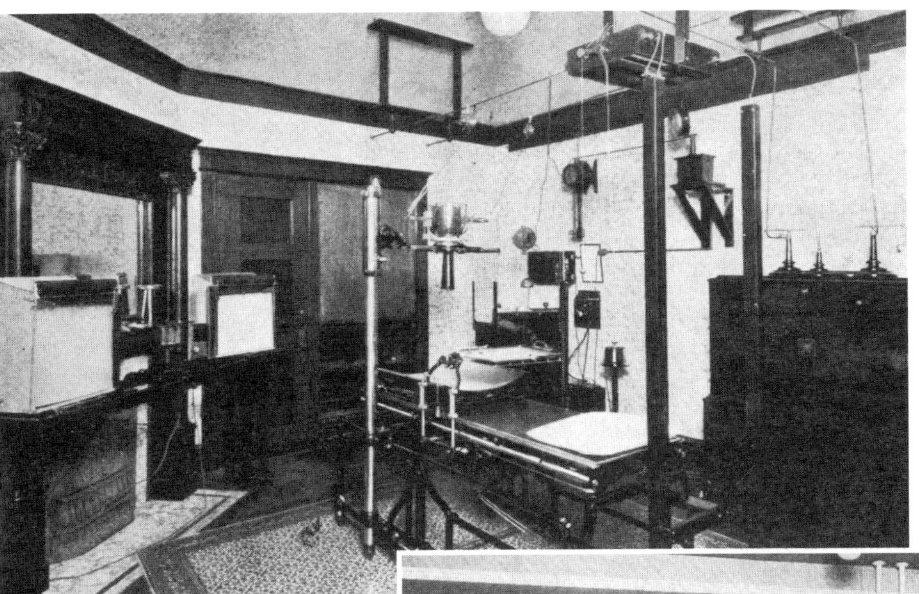

◀ X-Ray Lab

▲ Clinical Laboratory

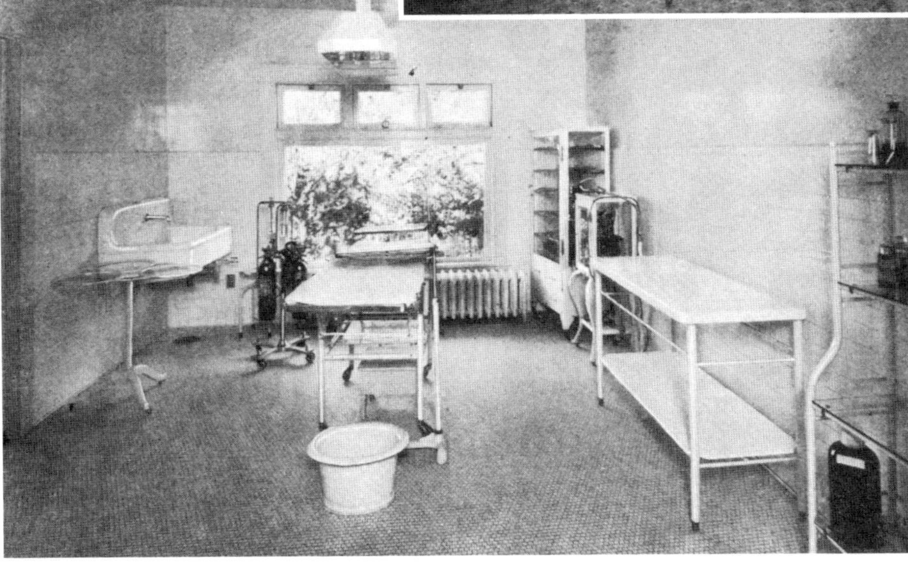

◀ Operating Room

Sponsored by Don and Madeline Davis

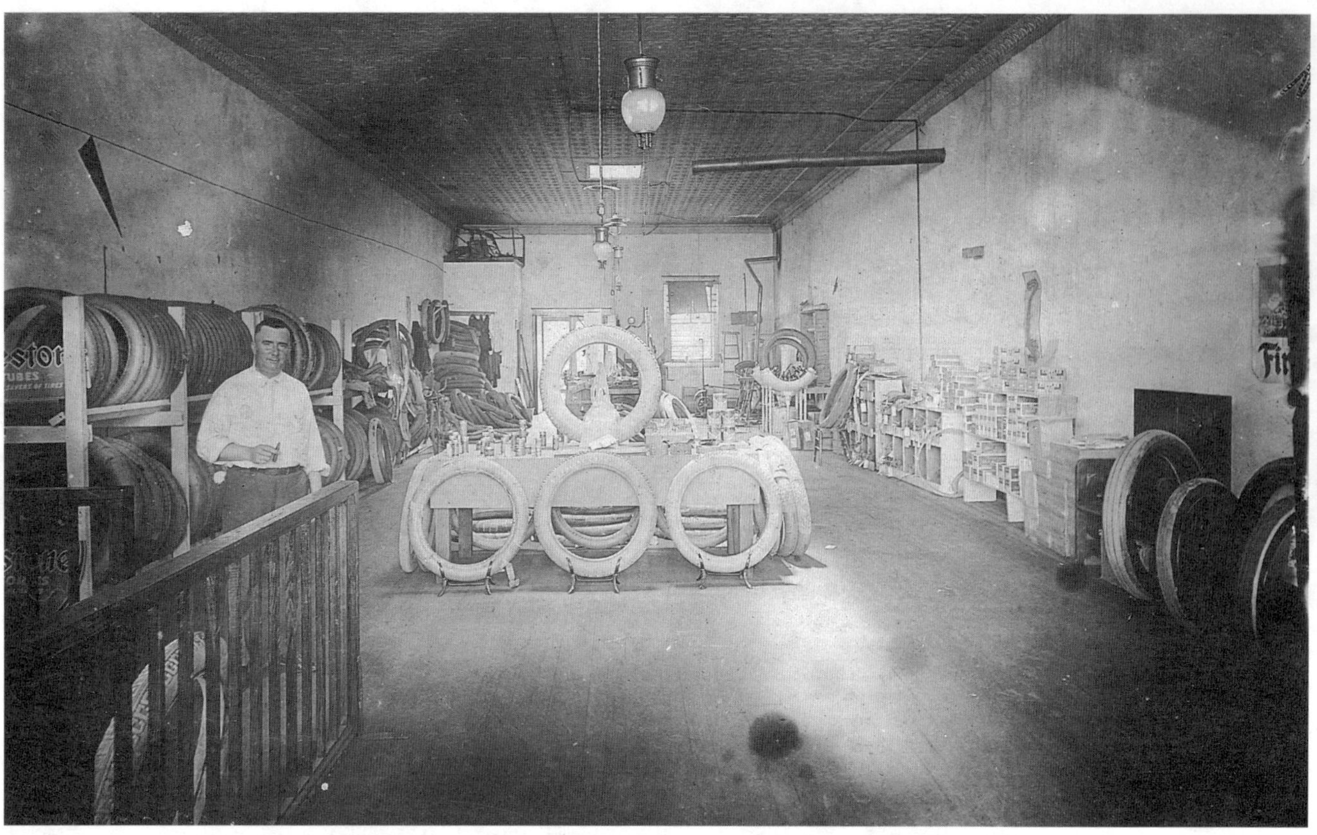

▲ John Crawford shown here, in the Crawford Garage and Machine Shop at 102 E. 4th Ave. in 1921.

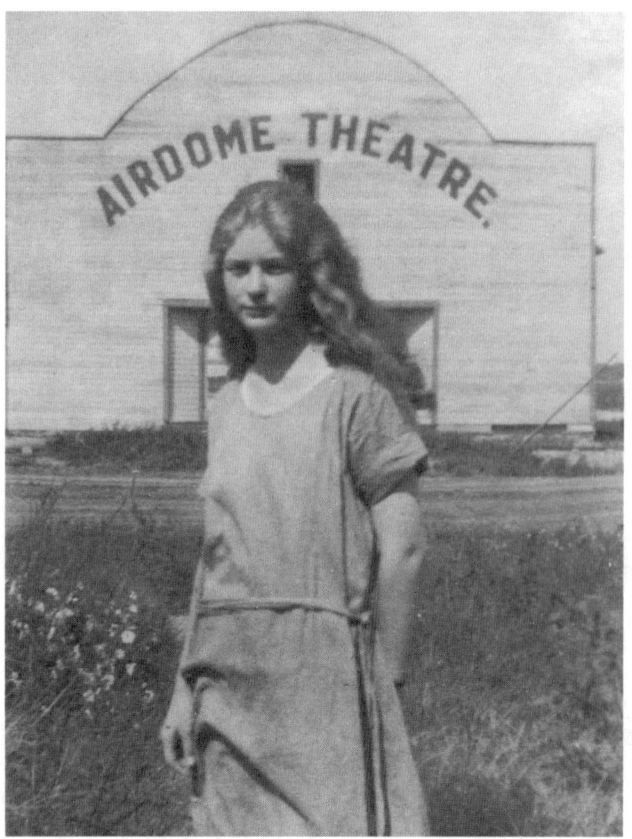

◀ Stella Chalmers is pictured in front of the Airdome Theater and skating rink in 1922. The airdome, built by E.R. Tarman in 1917, was located on the southwest corner of Oak & 5th. It was one hundred and fifty feet long and seventy five feet wide. There were no windows and ventilation came through openings along the sides, which had hinged covers. A stage was located on the west end, to be used for plays and a screen was in place to show the new moving pictures. Along the south side of the building was a duck pin alley. There were basketball goals and plenty of room for dancing and roller skating. Mr. Tarman wanted a swimming pool, so he hitched a team to a slip and gouged out a pit. For a lining he used stone, then built some small structures where people could change clothes. The Airdome continued in business until the depression of the thirties.

▲ The Thompson Brothers Grocery operated around 1920 in the Peckham building located in the 400 block of State Street. Shown are: the father of the brothers, I.T. Thompson (in dark suit); Russell Thompson (behind the counter); Jack Thompson (in apron), and an unidentified salesman.

▲ Students from Garfield School (K through 2nd Grade) at recess in October of 1922. Looking across the playground, toward High Street, you can see the edge of the High School, built in 1911 (then Jr. High). Between the playground and old high school is a concrete slab which was the original basketball court for the high school. There were no auditoriums and all basketball games were held out-of-doors.

Sponsored by Larry and Susie Wilkerson

▲ 54 Highway, east of Augusta, taken June of 1923.

▲ Looking east down 5th street from the corner of State. The 5th Avenue Hotel can be seen on the far left and the Opera Block on the far right. On the southeast corner, the Robson Department Store, was in business from the late 1800's, until closing in 1924, when the newly established American National Bank, moved into the building.

▲ Highway 54, west of Augusta before it was paved, at the old Whitewater River bridge.

Sponsored by Wal-Mart Store #346, 1618 N. Ohio

▲ A parade featuring members of the Rotary Baseball Team (left) and Kiwanis Baseball Team (Right) before their big game on June 23, 1922. To the far right is a large bull wearing a sign reading "This is no Bull, Kiwanis will win". The outcome of this eventful game is unknown.

▲ The state meeting of the Ku Klux Klan met in Augusta on September of 1923. The number of Klan members, from all over the state, numbered so high, they filled the street from curb to curb and extended from downtown to High Street.

Sponsored by Republic Supply Co., 409 Osage

▲ Peter Bausch Billards was located at 605 State St. in 1922.

▲ The First National Bank Building was located on the northeast corner of 5th and State, to the left was the Guest store, where cigars, sodas and tobacco were sold. To the far left was Dunn Mercantile Co. Note the street sign on the far left corner, it reads "Keep To The Right".

Sponsored by T & J Electric Inc., 413 School

▲ The First National Bank building after a tornado passed through Augusta in the evening hours of July 13, 1924.

▲ Looking from the center of the block just south of the school building, you can see the havoc left by the 1924 tornado. Not a house was left undamaged on this block. The pile of debris in the center is a dodge sedan twisted into pieces.

▲ What was left of this Model T-Ford following the storm.

▲ Damage to the Episcopal Church in the 200 block of Main.

▲ Employees of Spencer Trailer in its early years, when they were located in the 300 block of State St.

▲ An entry in the 4th of July Parade in the 1920's.

Sponsored by Heartland Plastics Inc., 910 Industrial Rd.

▲ Delores and Grover Phillips were the owners of PanTree Grocer in the late 1920's. Located at 529 State, it was one of the largest grocery stores in Augusta. On January 16, 1943, it was destroyed by fire.

◀ 1928 Augusta Girls Basketball Team: (Front Row L to R) Ruth Jester, Venita Ewalt, Audrey Wardrop; (2nd Row) Edith Falwell, Lela Rice, Vera Slayman, Madeline Skaer, Myrtle Pyle, Ethel Walton; (Back Row) Grace Bell, Walter Alstrom, Coach; Wilma Reid.

Sponsored by Augusta White Eagle Credit Union, 2105 Ohio

◀ The Federal Supply building (owner Ed Boggs) was located on the northeast corner of 5th and Santa Fe. This photo was taken during the 1928 flood.

▲ Employees of The Eureka Tool Co. located 1/4 mile south of Augusta in 1929; (L to R) John Owings, John C. Walworth, Ernest Keller, Ernest Wheeler.

Sponsored by Augusta White Eagle Credit Union, 2105 Ohio

▲ State Street, looking south during the 1920's, taken from a window in the upper stories of the Moyle Building.

▲ West side of the 500 Block of State Street looking south in the 1920's.

▲ Augusta Football Team, 1928: (Front Row L to R) Fred "Fritz" Mounts, Claude "Curly" Elliott, Frances "Bud" Moriarty, Dean "King" Kingsley, Wylie "Brick" Welter, Roy "Aggie" Agard (Middle Row) Orville "Hoppie" Hopkins, John "Rosie" Hime, Myron "Mac" McQuiston, Lonnie "Kemp" Kemper, Burl "Scotty" Scott, Gerald "Davy" Davis (Back Row) Chester "Chet" Pettibon, Gipson "Gip" Ralston, Dale "Fat" Murphy, Walter "Farmer" Ewalt, Norman "Sheik" Leitzke.

Sponsored by Kimberly, Audrey and Cassandra Wray

▲ This northward view from the Fifth & State intersection shows a car-lined commercial area with other drivers looking for a place to park and shop.

▲ Interior of the first Lehr's Cafe, located at 504 State St. in 1929. Standing (LtoR) are Charles and Thelma Lehr, Mrs. Jennings and Bernice Lehr. Seated are two unidentified men and two young boys, Jack Cox and Bob Tarman.

Sponsored by Village Decorative Shop, 117 W. 7th

1930-1940

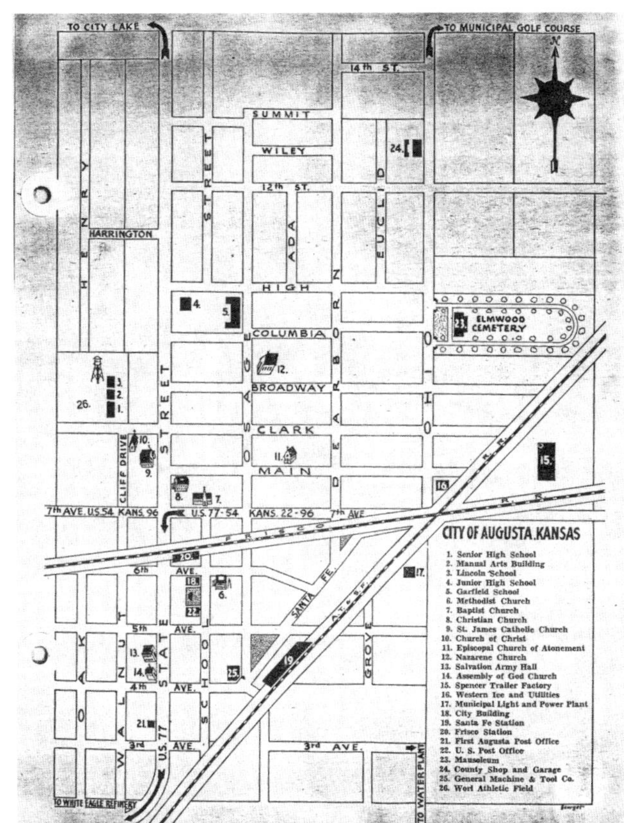

▶ Map of the city drawn in 1936 by Augustan John Bourget.

▲ The Praire State Bank first opened for business on December 4, 1918 at 512 State Street. On March 8, 1930, an extensive remodeling of the building was completed and the lobby was filled with bouquets of flowers in celebration of their updated facilities. The Praire State Bank was the only bank to survive and reopen following the bank holiday in 1933 and it remained Augusta's only bank until 1956.

▲ Augusta Volunteer Fire Department and Police Force in 1934. (Top Row L toR) Frank Lunsford, Unknown, R.O. Jackson, Charles Rawlings, Eldon Nordman, Tom Johnson, Harold Guest, Neal Jones, Charles Clippinger, G.C. Clem, Emerson Clippinger, John Hime, Willie Carlin, unknown. (Bottom Row) unknown, Chud Rice, unknown, C.B. Robb, Cecil Belscher, A.E. Pressnell, Paul Beard, Virgil Polk, George Burkhart, unknown.

▲ In 1923, Roy Schoeb built a Ford Dealership on the southeast corner of 7th and State. This new modern facility boasted an underground garage. In a front portion of the building was Fowler Service Station. Pictured here in front of the building are John and Randall Fowler, in 1935. On November 23, 1936, the entire Schoeb building was gutted when the roof burst into flames.

Sponsored by Brick Street Flower Co., 502 State St.

▲ Augusta Theater during construction in 1935.

▲ The Bisagno family came to Augusta in 1881 and settled on land northeast of town, where they were involved in farming, catttle buying and investing. A son, Dave Bisagno, entered the movie business in 1918, when he bought the Isis Theater at 521 State. In the following years, he also owned such theaters as the Mecca and the Liberty. On June 19, 1935, Dave and his wife Aline opened the Augusta Theatre at 523 State St. It became the architectural centerpiece of the community. It was the first theater to be lit entirely by neon. The facade of the theater was faced with individual tiles of Carrara structural glass and elaborate art deco interior includes ornamental plaster, canvas murals and stenciled ceiling. The theater, which is still in operation today, has played an important role in bringing entertainment and the arts to Augusta. Owned today by the Augusta Arts council, it has been placed on the National Register Of Historical Places.

▲ Dave Bisagno

▲ Aline Bisagno

▲ Kiwanis Drum and Bugle Corp, 1930's: (First Row) Marian Graham, Agnes Young, Leota Ewalt, Zeolah Buell, Alice Harryman, Carmen Boughton, Marjorie Dunsford, Leta Lester, Azela Patterson, Thelma Atkins (Second Row) Audrey Brewster, Mary Marlys Mallison, Carol Hurst, Edwina McIntosh, Maxine Twiggs, Madeline Dunsford, Fern Smith, Dorothy Liens, Delores Davis, Inez Morris, Frances Walker.

▲ Aubrey Martin pictured in front of the Standard Station on the southwest corner of 7th and State in 1935. The building later became the Shryock Oil Co. In 1954.

Sponsored by Cooper Drug, Inc., 509 State St., - Cletus Kappelmann

▲ Rawlings Tire and Electric Service, owned by Charles Rawlings, was open for business from 1932 to 1946. It was located on the north side of the 100 block of east 6th street. They specialized in auto repair and sold tires and batteries.

▲ Fowler Service Station, 7th and Osage in 1936.

▲ 1937 Police and Fire Department: (LtoR) Chief Roy "Blondie" Mercer, Vern Dix, Claude Chappell, Chud Rice, Pete Peterson, George Lietzke

▲ The Rebekah Lodge Degree Team (Back Row LtoR) Pearl Burnett, Lula Bankey, Thelma Lehr, Lottie Koons, Jennie Reed, Sarah Porter, Cora Holt, Teresa Rawlings, Clara Wilford, Dova Tagtmeyer, Ada Rice (Front Row) Anna McDuffee, Carrie Young, Effa Wheat, Flora Tripp, Grace Thompson, Clara Moody, Alice Smith, Alice Hobbs, Kate Stevens, Laura May Huston

▲ Audna Reeves school class in 1937 (Front Row) Dick Mauk, unknown, Phillip Spencer, Jack Patterson, Rosetta Cox, Betty Shield (Second Row) Mary Kay Millison, Alan Cobb, Billy Young, Oscar York, Ada Beth Scalph, Carmelita Moser, Pauline Jordan (Third Row) Burrell Burgess, David West, Homer Berner, Wilbur Gardner, Marilyn Mardis, Ronald Williams, Lupe Cabrales (Fourth Row) Bobby Hobbs, Jim Firebaugh, unknown, unknown, Wanda Cowan, Barbara Sweeney, unknown.

◀ For many years the United States Post Office building was located at 509 School street. The building is currently being used as an apartment house.

▲ On December 29, 1938 the new Post Office building, on the south west corner of 5th and School, opened for their first day of business.

◀ Lehr's Restaurant moved from the 500 block of State to this building at 634 State around 1939-1940. Two years later the building was sold and moved to Douglas Avenue in Wichita, Kansas.

Sponsored by Barbara Mickle Brown

1940-1950

▲ The "Flying Red Horses" (Socony-Vacuum) winning baseball team of the 1940's: (L to R) John Fowler, Manager; Waldon Reed, Ralph Kipers, Wade Moriarty, Kenneth Dill, Friday Murray, Clark Hartman, Raymond Blanden, A.Z. Seaman, Lawrence "Mutt" Cornelius, Harold Obenchain, Chester "Chet" Powers, Cliff Singer, Ed Mehl, Jack Hegleson, Theral "Catt" Leedom, Herb Coin, Ass't Manager. (boy in front kneeling is unknown)

▲ Employees of Spencer Trailer in 1940-41. (Back Row L to R) Earl L. Mercer, Ralph High, Durrell Davis, Fred Spencer, Elmer Hathorn, Harry Waymire, Frank Jones, unknown, Walter Book, unknown, Henry Lentz, Hubert Femster, Bill Eldringhoff, Marion Spencer, Jim Justice, unknown, unknown, Lee cody, Evert Jones, Bob Curren, Lowell Penington, Fred Ortman, Audine Miller (Front Row) Charlie Prigle, Henry Neihardt, Orley Bonnom, Ralph Sapp, Creason, John Wheeler, Harold Harrison, John Spencer, Willie Carlin.

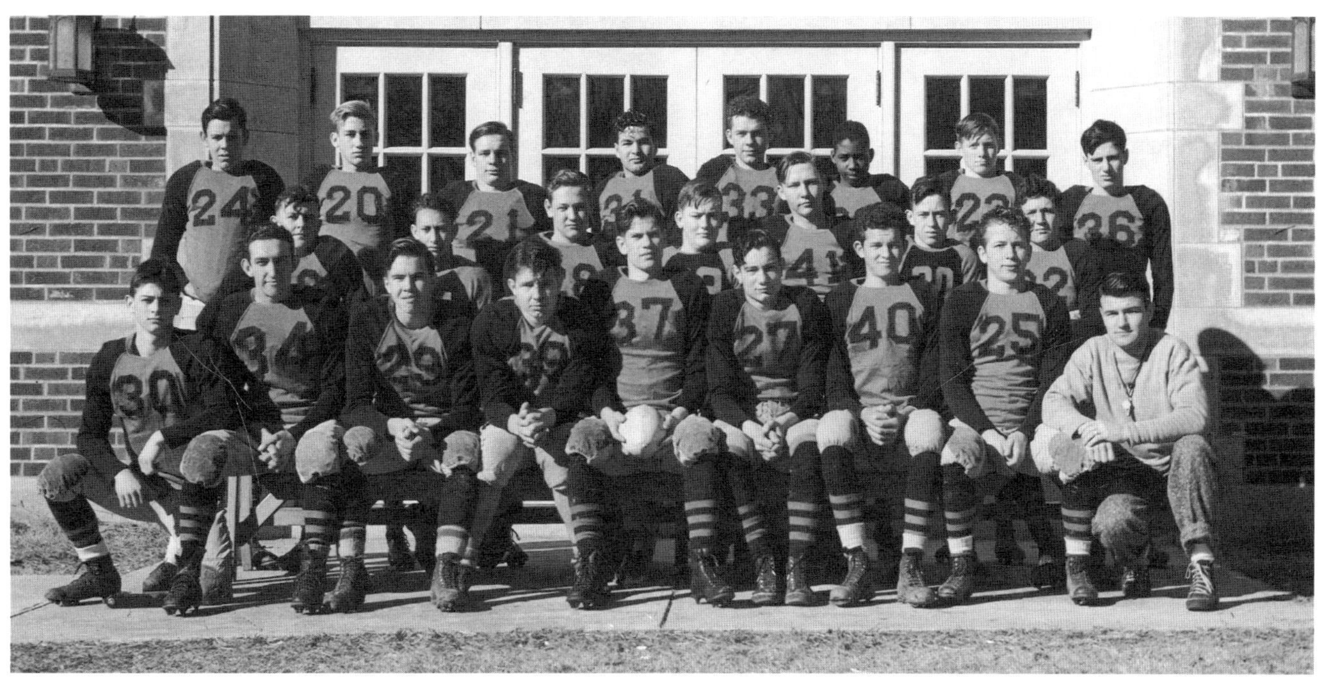

▲ This was the last high school football team to play in the fall of 1941, before World War II started in December. Most of the seniors were in the military by the next fall. (Back Row L to R) Buster "gitter bug" Mann, Bob Guest, Grey "Irish" Ward, Calvin "Apple" Applegate, Tom Trotter, Herman Reed, Max Dye, Gerald "Lefty" Burns (Middle Row) John " Little Patsy" Clark, Paul "Dude" Kaylor, Lawrence "Junior" Kennedy, John Mercer, Lee Lenz, Sherman Parry, Dean "Lard" Myers (Front Row) Bob "Driller" Garden, Charles "Shickew" Shipmon, Paul LeSeur, Jim Clinger, Wallace "Wash" Fowler, Maurice Rowe, Buster "Buz" Bechtold, Lawrence "Tubby" Smith, Coach David Shirk.

▲ West side of the 500 block of State Street, looking northwest, in the early 1940's

Sponsored by Pigeon's Roost Mall, 601 State St.

▲ Garvin Park in the 1940's —Entrance to the park.

▲ Dam

▲ Picnic area

▲ Bridge across the creek

▲ Overview taken from the dam

Sponsored by Dean and Georgie Skaer

▲ State street looking south from the corner of 7th and State.

▲ 400 block of State Street, looking south from 5th street, in the 1940's. Notice the flags hanging from all the storefronts.

Sponsored by Dillons Stores, 1510 Ohio

▲ In 1949, the 54 Motor Company owned by Nevelyn Rawlings and Eldon Tarman, was located at 310 West 7th. Just to the west of 54 Motor was a small diner called Vans Burger Bar and then on further was the Dairy Queen.

▲ Looking toward the east of 54 Motor Company was the skating rink owned by Maggie and Ray Prigmore and later purchased by Calvin Applegate.

▲ State Street looking north from the middle of the 400 block. Safeway Grocery and Calverts Department Store can be seen on the left.

▲ Santa Fe Depot in the 1940's.

Sponsored by Dillons Stores, 1510 Ohio

▲ Augusta residents look to the south of downtown, as a tornado passes by in the air.

▲ Augusta was the first city in the United States to raise sufficient funds for the building and launching of a fighting rescue boat during World War II. A wartime , bond-stamp fundraising campaign was started here on February 24, 1943 and completed about a month later. The rescue craft #20982 christened the "Augusta" had a cruising range of 600 miles and a crew of seven. It evacuated hundreds of isolated and wounded guerilla fighters from the East Indies and the Philippines. It was also called a Sea Horse as it could go where sea rescue planes could not go. With its own gun batteries, it could shoot its way out of trouble while rescuing Army Air Force pilots shot down near enemy bases.

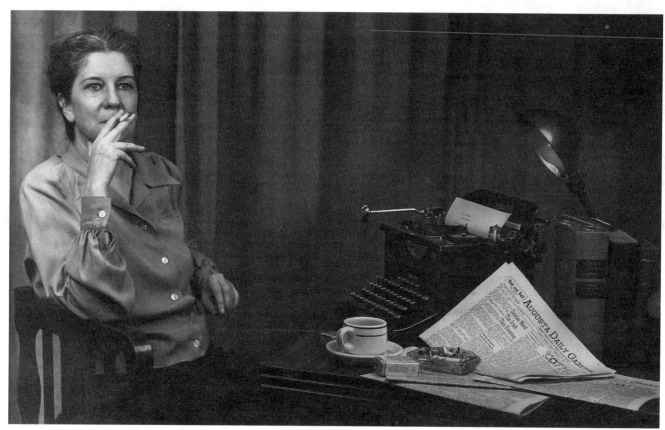

▲ Bert Shore, editor of the Augusta Daily Gazette, was the first woman inducted into the Kansas Newspaper Hall of Fame. She and her brother, Chet, had purchased the Gazette in 1928. Bert became well known for her popular column, "Half and Half".

▲ 1943 State Champion Orioles Basketball Team: (Back Row LtoR) Junior Crowder, Bill Sapp, Larry Kennedy, Sherman Parry, Glenn Fillmore and Bob Watt (Front Row) David Erwin, Homer Smotherman, Marion Robison, M.C. Ewart and Coach Dave Shirk.

Sponsored by Dillons Stores, 1510 Ohio

▲ Several of the boys who graduated from the class of 1944, immediately joined the Navy. Home on leave after Boot Camp, they met in the park for a picnic and were joined by friends from other branches of the service.(LtoR) Meridith Shryock, John Mercer, Kenneth Ludlam, Jim Quest, Charles Burns, Bob Watt, Milo McNairy, Homer Rippee, Dick Wintermote, Willie Patterson, Dick Dunsford, Richard Bartholomew, Sherman Parry, Ward Parry, Earl Mercer, Monroe Cox.

▲ Scholfield Hatchery was located at 417 State from 1941 to 1949. Wayne Dewing and Gene Scholfield are behind the counter.

▲ Saturday afternoon at the Augusta Theater in the 1940's.

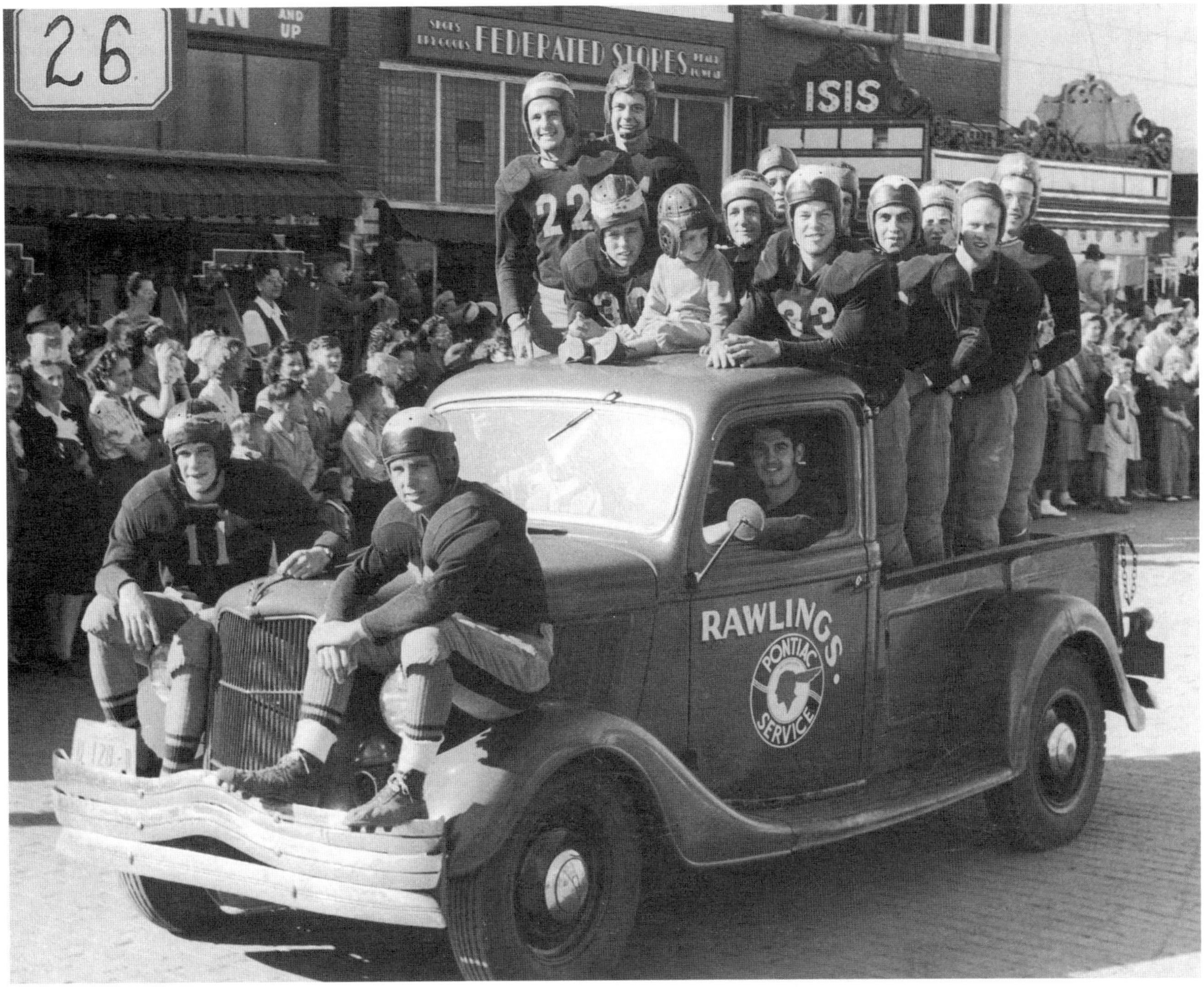

▲ Augusta High Schools Football Team, in the Diamond Jubilee Parade in 1946 (Citywide 75th Celebration). (Front Row) Bob Sapp, Dick Ward, Alan Cobb, (Second Row) Bob Kennedy, Hutter, Cliff Boucher, Lupe Cabrales, O.D. Sapp (Third Row) Corky Smith, Gene Saliday, Gene Reece, Jack Guest, Ray Stevens, Bill January, Jim Firebaugh

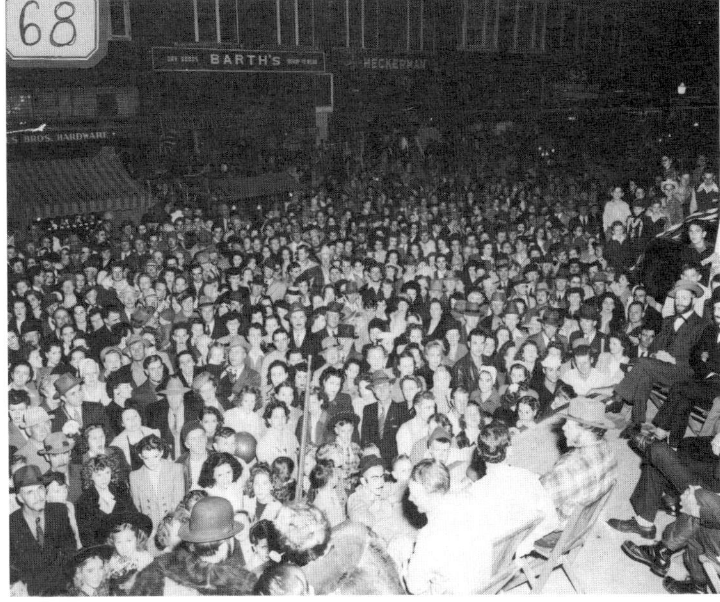

▶ Augustan's and friends packed the streets of Augusta during the Diamond Jubilee for the town's 75th anniversary in July of 1946.

Sponsored by Stockton Memorials, 1004 Ohio

◄ Winners of the Diamond Jubilee Beard Contest were Vernon Gustafson, Warren Proctor, Harold Jones and Fred "Pop" Duvanel.

▲ Diamond Jubilee Parade, July 1946, taken looking northeast in the 500 block of State street.

Sponsored by C.A. Cook and Sons, 714 Ohio

◀ By 1941, restoration of the C.N. James Log Cabin was completed and the interior of the cabin housed the Augusta Historical Museum. Stella B. Haines, Historical Society and Museum founder, along with J.J. Manion and Mrs. Holladay, show off the museum during the 1947 Diamond Jubilee.

▲ The J. & D. Department Store was located at 515 State Street from 1947 to 1952. Emma Johnson (L) was co-owner of the store and Beatrice Clinger (R) was clerk.

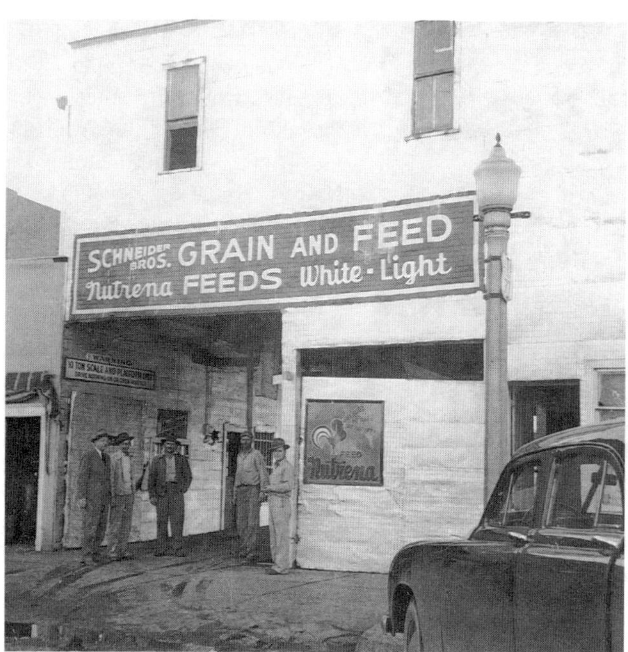

▲ Schneider Brothers Grain and Feed at 617 State Street. Owners Lorenzo Schneider (2nd from left) and Frank (far right) Schneider, stand in front of the building.

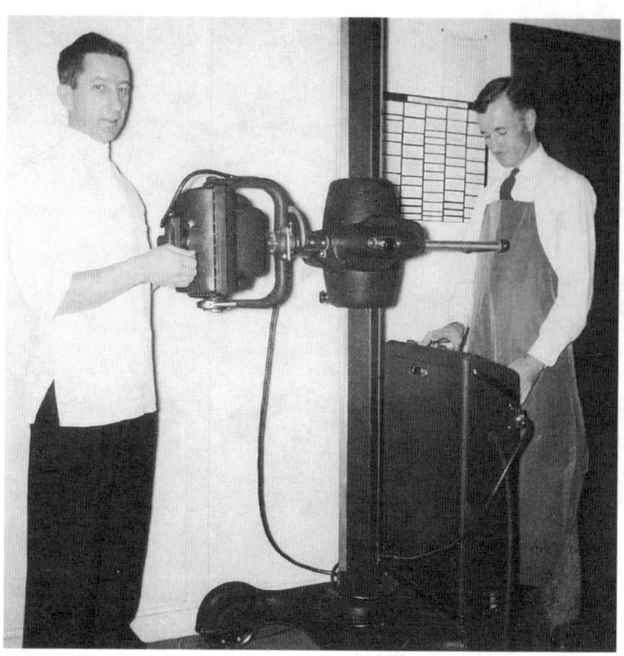

▲ Dr. Glenn E. Colvin and Dr. Weldon R. Gentzler opened a new chiropractic office in November of 1948 at 106 W. 6th.

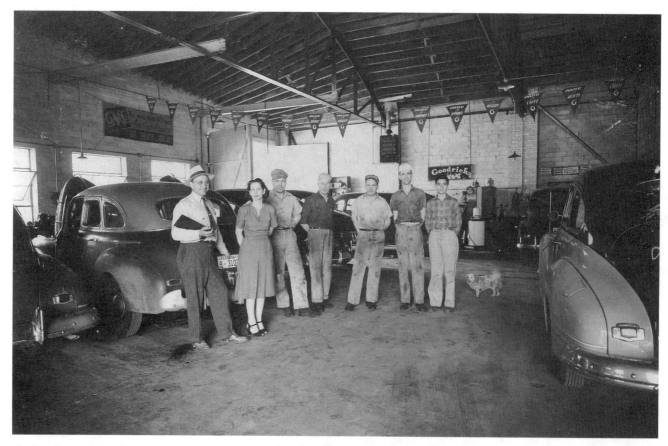

▲ Rawlings Motor Service at 401 State Street sold Pontiac cars, GMC trucks and Case Tractors from 1947 to 1955. Shown left to right: Charles Rawlings, Tressa Rawlings, Nevelyn Rawlings, Jim Kimble, Eldon Tarman, Harold Willing and Stan Rawlings.

Sponsored by Charlotte's Family Hairstyling, 1008 Ohio

1950-1960

▲ John Moyle donated land on the northeast corner of Kelly and Dearborn, for the city to build a municipal pool. The pool opened in the spring of 1951.

◀ A stadium full of Augusta supporters, like Dick Pennington and Dorothy Burris shown in the background, get 'the spirit' from the 1950 Augusta High Cheerleaders: (LtoR) Edith Alfaro, Joyce Wilson, Jo Ann Jones, Billie Mallory.

▲ In April of 1951, a small shanty town developed around the old sewage disposal plant south of town.

▲ "The World's Most Deserted Cemetery" was the title given by the Augusta Gazette, when they ran this picture on April 14 of 1951. It was taken atop the ridge between the city and the small shanty town located around the old sewage disposal plant. In an area enclosed by board posts and sagging barb wire were 3 graves marked "Unknown Babies", dated 1937.

Sponsored by Like A Rose, 343 Main

▲ Twirlers, (LtoR) Leota Scott, Sara Kemper and Jennice Martin, performed at high school games and led the Augusta Orioles Band in 1950.

◀ Bert Shore, co-editor of the Augusta Gazette, enjoys a moment with the gazette newsboys in 1951: (Back) Jack Dornbusch; (Middle) Arlin Miller, Buddy Obenchain, Lee Miller, Bill Gardner, Gary Burkhart (Front) Jim Garrison, Ron Hatchett.

▲ Fred Spencer first opened Spencer Trailer in 1916, in the blacksmith shop owned by his father-in-law, HB Walker, in the 300 block of State Street. The business grew and expanded until he built a new building in 1927 for $150,000.00, east of town at the railroad junction. Pictured here in an aerial view in 1950, the business continued to operate very successfully for many years.

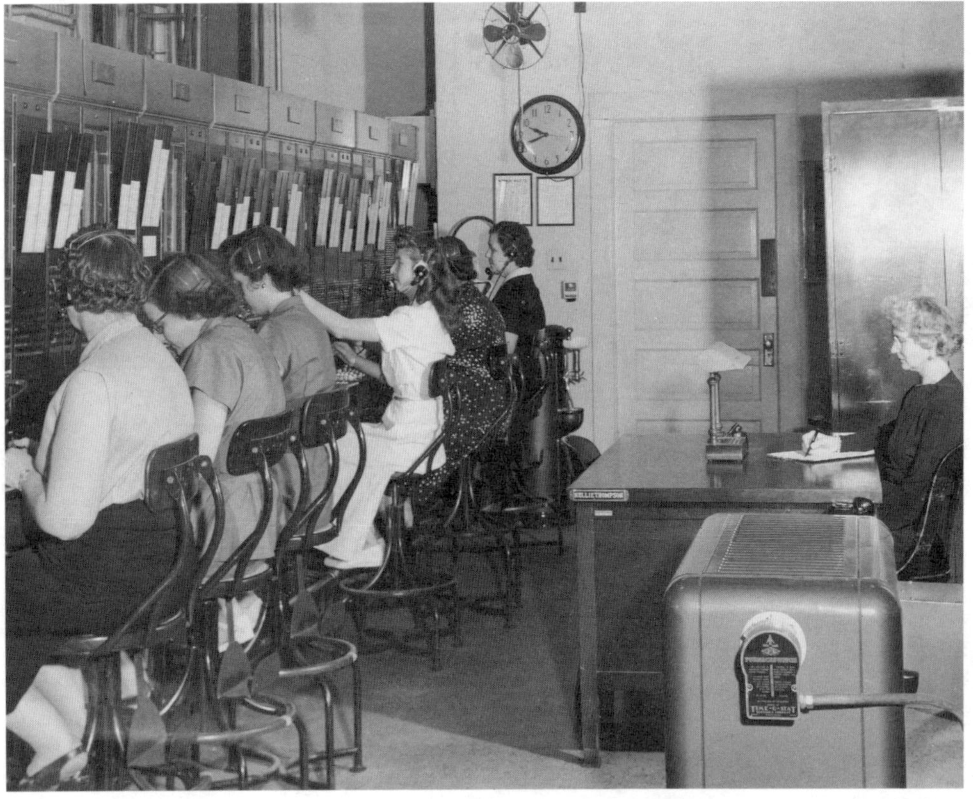

◀ The Southwestern Bell telephone operators at work in their office at 416 State in April of 1951: (L to R) Alta Hamilton, Jerry Jones, Jean Trebbe, Mildred Matlock, Minnie Doyle, Velma Obenchain, Nellie Thompson.

▲ The Southwestern Bell Telephone crew and some of their families taken in the fall of 1952 (Front L. to R.) Shirley Johnson, Olive Moreland, Sally Tuttle, Alta Hamilton, Jack Thompson, Nellie Thompson, Vivian Davis, Virginia Cody, Jean Trebbe (Back) Betty Hanshaw, Gerald Timmons, Dorothea Bing, Everett Davis, Joretta Davis, Bud Hanshaw, Ted Purcell.

▲ Looking North on State Street from the 400 block in 1950.

Sponsored by Madrigal and Associates, Inc., 109 E. 5th St.

Boys' Foods

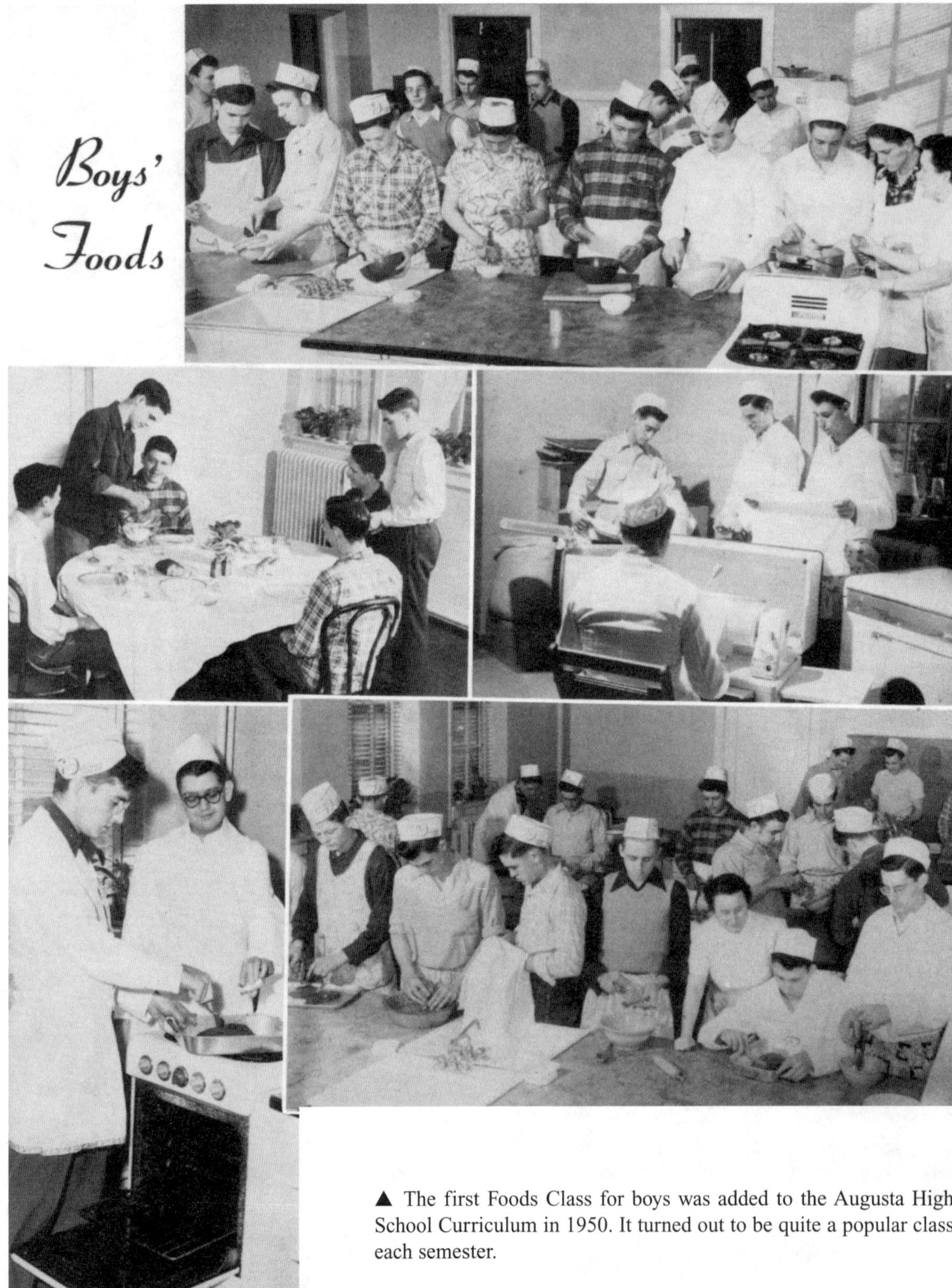

▲ The first Foods Class for boys was added to the Augusta High School Curriculum in 1950. It turned out to be quite a popular class each semester.

Sponsored by Nations Bank, N.A. of Augusta, 645 State St.

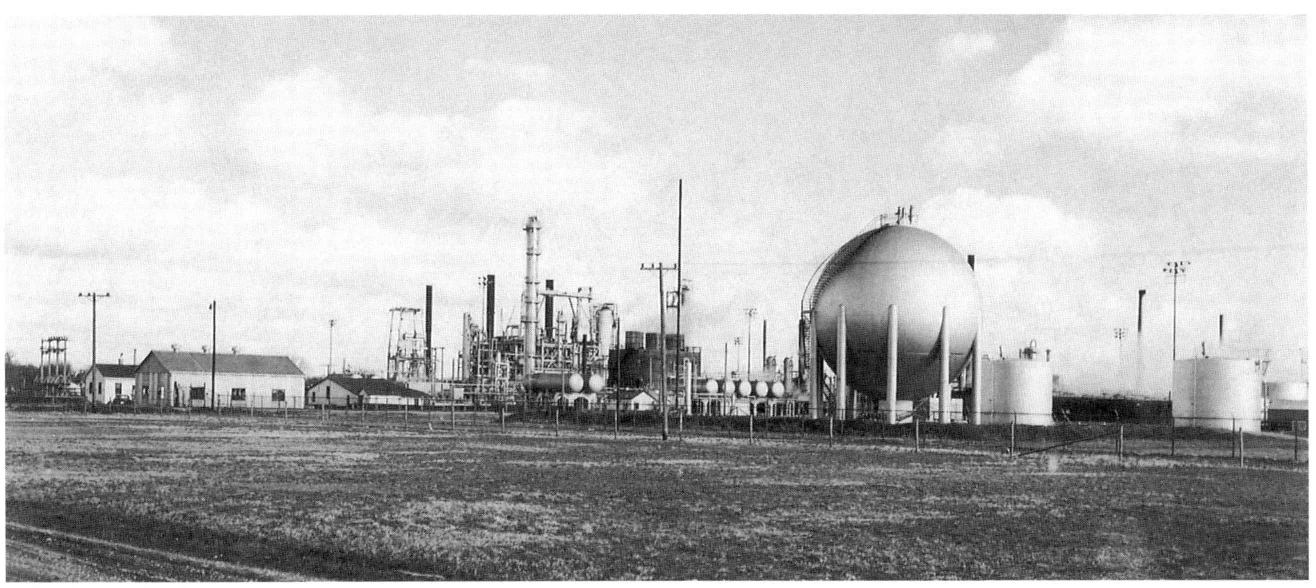

▲ Socony-Vacuum Refinery in the 1950's.

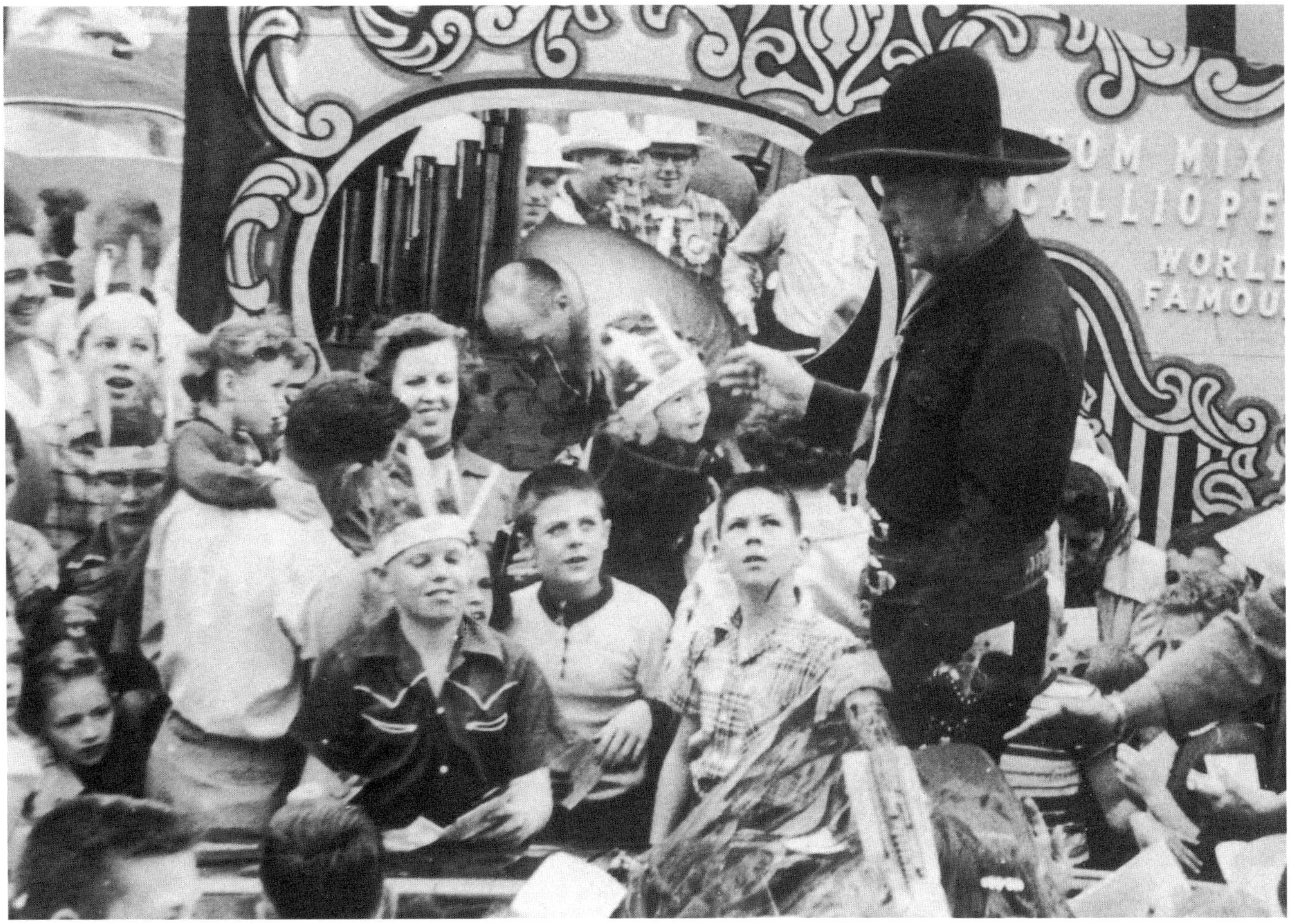

▲ It was a big day in Augusta when Hopalong Cassidy came to town to promote his film. Children and grown-ups alike crowded the sidewalk in front of the Augusta Theater hoping for a chance to visit with Hopalong. Accompaning him was actress Gloria Graham.

Sponsored by Three French Hens, 610 School and Gore-Evans Gallery, 616 School St.

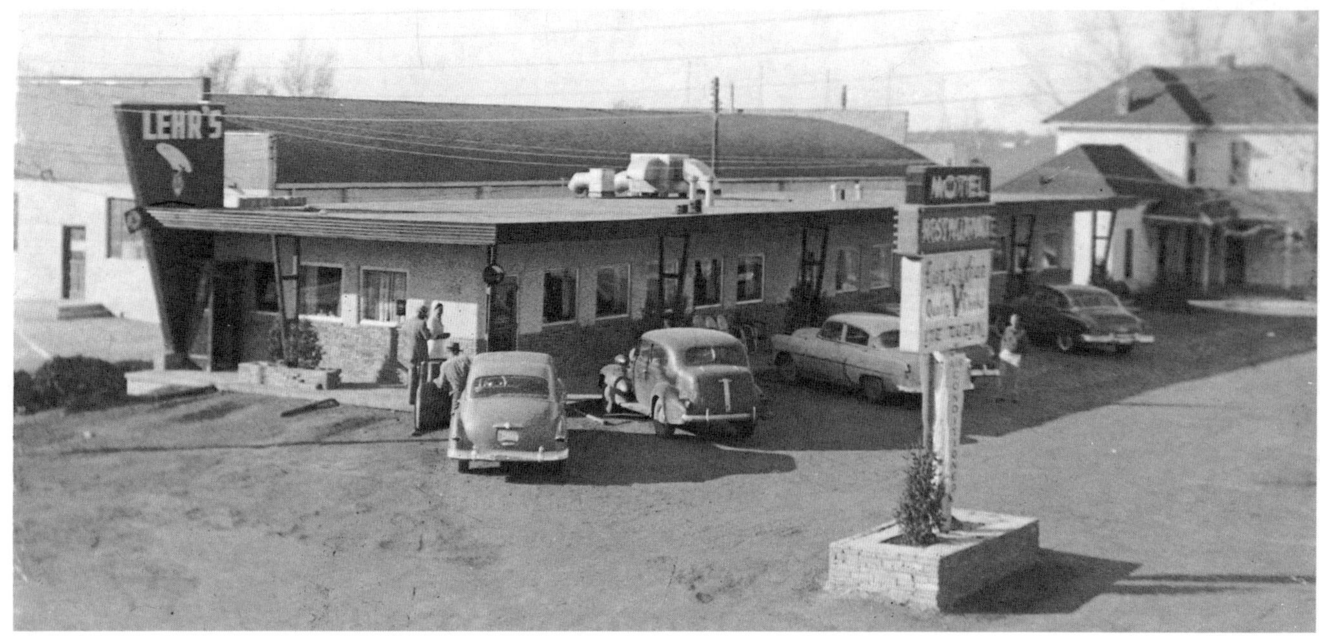

▲ By 1954, Lehr's had remodeled the interior of the skating rink, located in the 300 block of West 7th St., into a family style restaurant. It had a small stage toward the front of the building, which they used for melodrama's. Right along side the restaurant they built the Lehr's Motel.

▲ Members of the Board of Education in 1955: Vernon Gustafson, H.H. Robinson, (V.Pres) Pauline Bostwick, (Pres.) Dean Skaer, Virgil Simpson, Irene Welch, Warren Proctor, W.M. Henrick.

▶ A celebration of the 35th anniversary of the Twentieth Century Club was held on February 15 of 1958 in the home of C.O. Varner. (Front Row LtoR) Mrs. R.O. Ralston, Mrs. Aubra Sander, Mrs. Leonard Brown, Mrs. Henry Cordes; (Middle Row) Mrs. Ed Lietzke, Mrs. F.H. Varner, Mrs. C.O. Varner, Mrs. C.W. McVickers, Mrs. Effie Rigg Swegle, Mrs. Helen Etnire, Mrs. G.P. Skaer, Mrs. J.F. Dunsford, Mrs. John R. Crowley Jr.; (Back Row) unknown, unknown, Mrs. Irving Lenz, Mrs. S.T. Johnston, Mrs. W.D. Thomas, Mrs. D.A. Bisagno, Mrs. Emory Skinner, Miss Mayme Kibbey, Mrs. Charles Dine, Mrs. A.D. Manka, Mrs. Walter Cox, Mrs. Anna McCracken

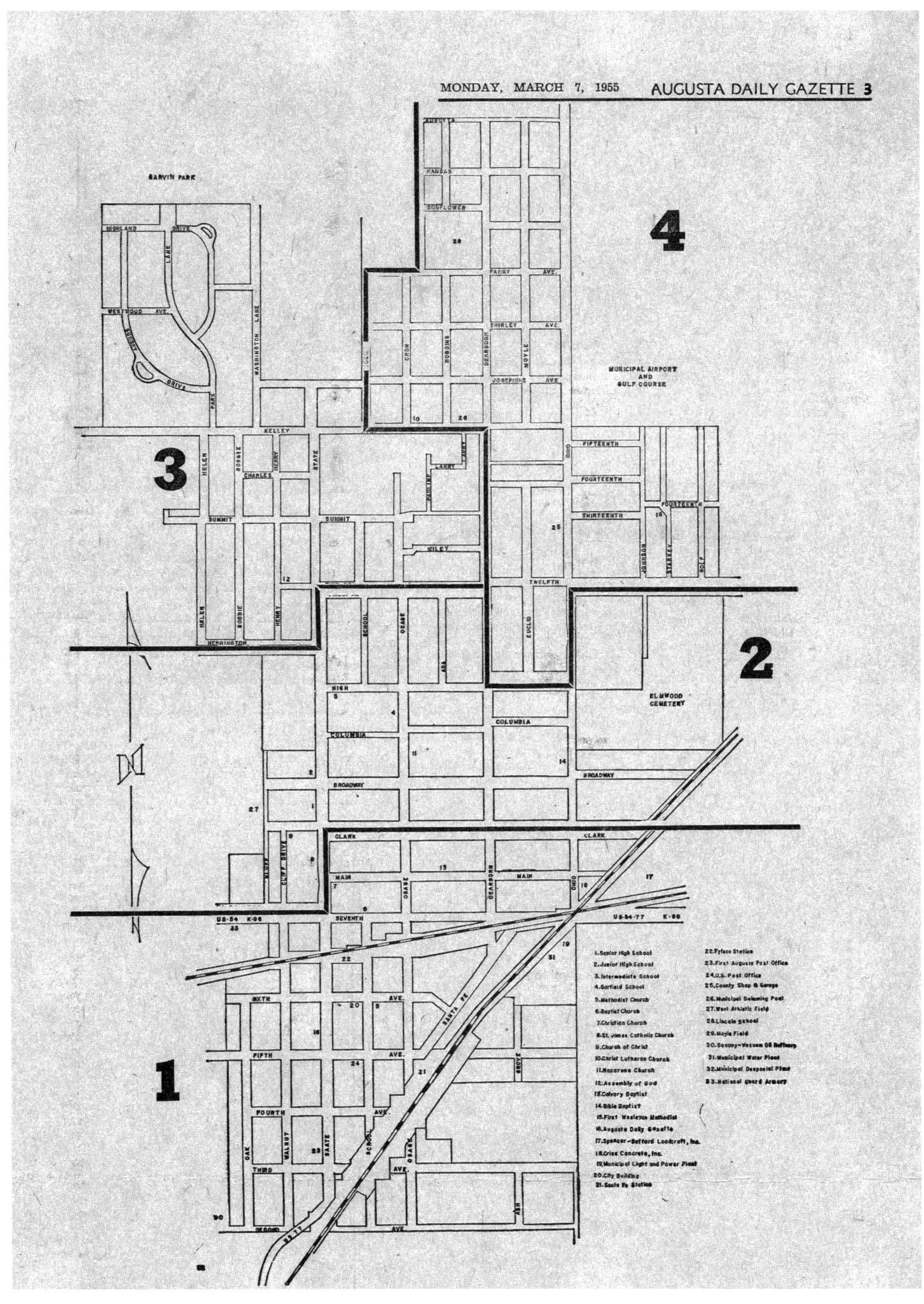

▲ Plat of Augusta, 1955

Sponsored by Frye Chevrolet Ranch, 603 W. 7th

▲ The local Chapter Beta Sigma, of Epsilon Sigma Alpha International in April 1959. (Back LtoR) Marjorie Rich, Evelyn Schurr, Pat McClure, Glenda Boucher, Joyce Gurney, Darlene Scholfield, Gloria Wager, Virginia Belt, Dorothy Burress, Violet Crowe (Front) Lucille Bolze, Phyllis Jolly, Nancy Wakeling, Betty McMilkan, Norma Bartholomew, Gerry Pouncey.

◀ The Hoskinson Animal Clinic at 704 Belmont was opened in 1959 by Dr. Glenn Hoskinson. It was the first animal clinic established in Augusta.

1960-1968

▲ The Oil Chemical and Atomic Workers Ladies Auxiliary 5246A dedicated a new Veterans Honor Roll on Memorial Day, May 30, 1960. The honor roll of W.W. II and the Korean War contained over 1000 names. The new honor roll was to replace the old one that had been put on the Elks building during the war years and was later accidentally destroyed. (Front Row L To R) Ivan Rich, Billie Butler, Barbara Butts, Bertha Shore, Goldie Larcom, Commander Verner C. Smith; (Back Row) Lyle Freeman, Lynn Hurd, Ralph Grady, Howard Larcom, Bill Lytton, John Wheeler, and Clyde Norton. The honor roll is present today on the north side of the Style Shop at 503 State Street.

Sponsored by Wayne and Jane Mathias and by Sherman and Nina Swan Parry

▲ Socony Oil Company Refinery became the Mobil Oil Company in 1966.

▲ A parade for the South Butler County Fair was held in Augusta on August 13, 1960. Ercel Mickle of Mickle Service and Farm Equipment, shows off his newest line of tractors.

▲ In 1965, members of the Augusta Boy Scouts and their leaders attended Philmont Scout Ranch in Cimarron, New Mexico. (Top Row L to R) Bill Grist, David Wentz, Darrell Markley, Greg Miller, Jay Weiss, Jon Weiss, Mike Malone, Brian Simmons, Don Deaton; (Middle Row) Sam Crook, Steve Buskirk, Louis Weiss, Don Wentz, Mike Buskirk, John Mills, Harry Buskirk, Greg Ewalt, Jerry Hubbart; (Bottom Row) Leroy Anderson and Steve Hammond.

◀ Vicky Lunger was crowned Miss Kakeland in 1965 by actress Vera Miles.

▲ Calverts Department Store opened in 1927 in the north building of the Viets Department Store at 431 State. In 1930, Viets closed and Calverts took over the remainder of the building. Very popular with both locals and out of towners, it soon became "The Place To Shop" in Augusta.

▲ John Cooper, pharmacist (Right), went to work for Grant Drug Store in 1911. In 1922, he opened Cooper Drugstore at 523 State. Pictured here Cletus Kappelmann, who eventually bought Cooper Drug, is presenting John with a certificate from the Pharmaceutical Association in recognition of John's over 50 years of service.

▲ In the mid 1960's, the Augusta Historical Society met to discuss the construction of a new museum building just south of the historical log cabin. (Top Row L To R) Morris Moon, John Mercer, Charles Heilman, Lee Gish, and L.E. Hundemer. (Third Row) Mrs. Robert Puckett, Mrs. Cecil Kirch, Mrs. Paul Kinnamon and Mrs. Robert Wright (Second Row) Mrs. E.A. Pouncey, Merle E. Driggs, Eldon "Pop" Nordman, and Mrs. Nordman (Front Row) John West, Mrs. West, Mrs. Marion Alley, Mrs. Gladys Shearer, and Mrs. Vivian Woody.

Sponsored by Chuck Korte Real Estate & Auction Service, Inc., 139 S. Hwy. 77

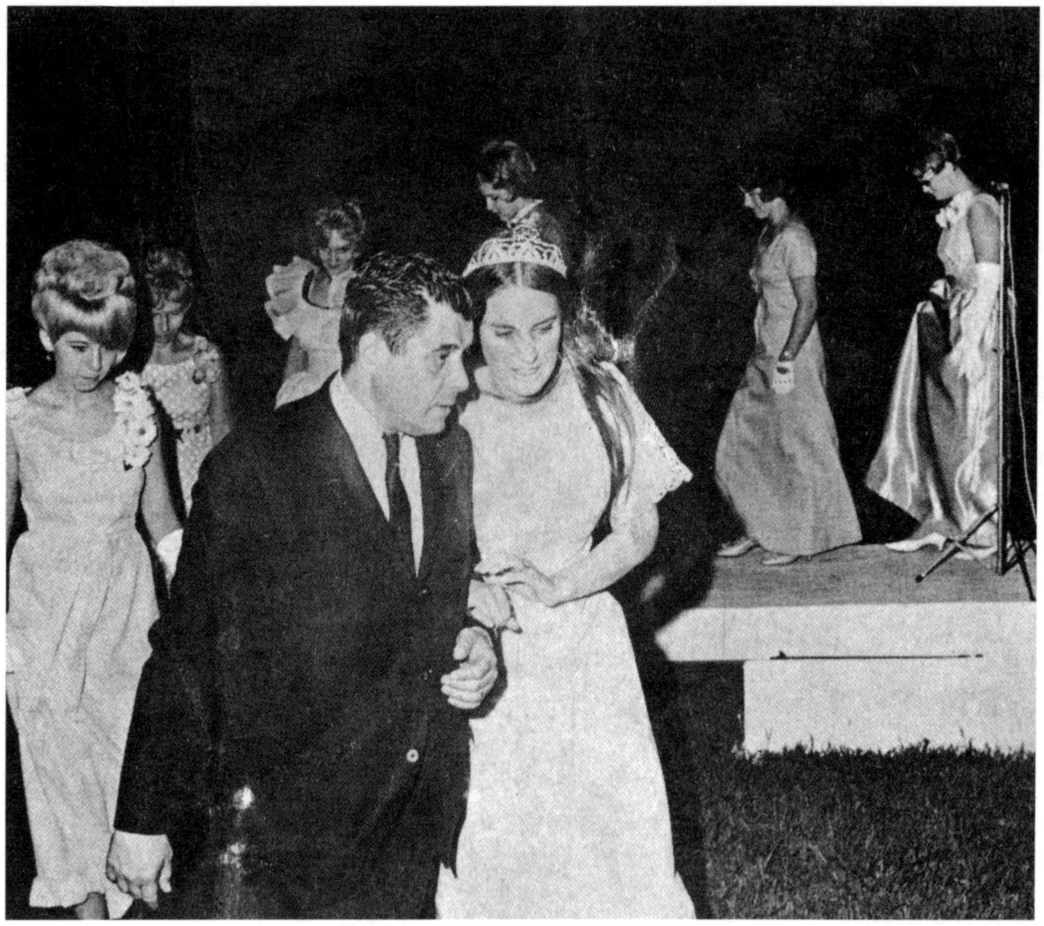

▲ Paulette Lonneke was crowned Miss Augusta, during the Centennial Celebration in 1968. She was escorted off stage by the then Kansas Govenor Robert Docking. Runners-up were Judy Maddox, Ethelyn Goodwin, Dwalia Britton, Jean Walton, Marilyn Ayres and Janice Schaible.

▶ The Centennial Celebration Parade kicked off on August 24, 1968 with Mayor Lee Dennett and Berlin Cox riding in a 1908 Reo. They were followed by other old car enthusiasts, floats representing the lives of the pioneers, and a lot of music by several different bands

Sponsored by Bill and Evie Shriver and by Eldon and Doylene Foreman

▲ Glenn Cunningham and youngsters parade a water buffalo.

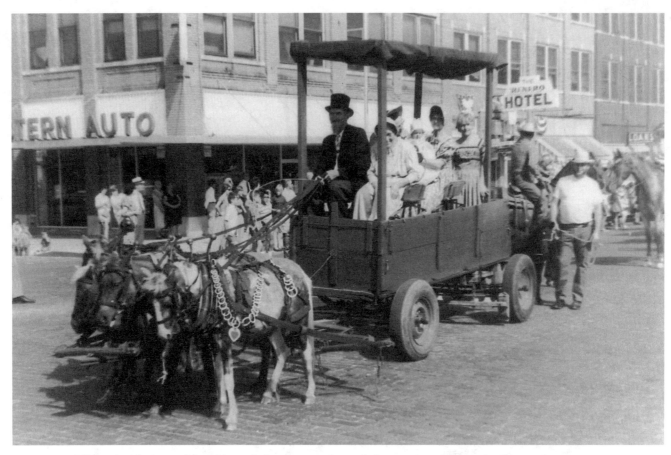

▲ Harry Uhlig and wife Rose, dressed in period costumes, drove their wagon and horses in the parade.

▶ The 'Centennial Bells' rode down state street in a wagon pulled by horses (L to R) Billie Butler, Dixie Fisher, Paula and Miriam Mann, Shirley and Sabrnia Lietzke, Marie Wakefield, Ruth Ann Tipton and Helen Stevens.

Sponsored by Nothing Ordinary Bake Shop, 503 State St.